The Master of Love

- Book Three -

E. G. White

Remnant
Publications

Coldwater, MI

Cover art by
Darrel Tank

Cover Design by
David Berthiaume

Master of Love
This edition published 2015

Printed in the United States of America

ISBN 978-1-933291-68-0

This book has been compiled from selected chapters of the
book *The Desire of Ages*.

ARE YOU SEARCHING FOR TRUTH?

Do you need reliable answers to urgent questions?

- *Can we know and understand the future?*
- *What are the tests of a true prophet?*
- *Is the development of character important?*
- *Are there physical and spiritual laws for health and happiness?*
- *What really happens to us after death?*
- *Is it possible to live forever?*
- *How can you find inner peace in a world of chaos?*

Discover the answers to these and other vital questions by enrolling in our Bible Correspondence Course. We care about you and your welfare. Thats why we prepared this series of thought-provoking Bible study lessons to help people just like you. These lessons will stimulate you to think independently, and help you conscientiously make the choices which will make you happy.

The first two lessons in the series are free of charge. If you like the lessons, we ask you to include a nominal freewill offering, beginning with lesson three, to help cover postage and handling.

Do You Want To Know More?

Yes, Please send me, at no charge, the first two lessons.

Name _____

Address _____

City _____ State _____ Zip _____

Send to:

Bible Correspondence Course
P.O. Box 426
Coldwater, MI 49036   ML 10

Contents

1

"Give Ye Them to Eat"

This chapter is based on Matthew 14:13-21; Mark 6:32-44; Luke 9:10-17; John 6:1-13.

C hrist had retired to a secluded place with His disciples, but this rare season of peaceful quietude was soon broken. The disciples thought they had retired where they would not be disturbed; but as soon as the multitude missed the divine Teacher, they inquired, "Where is He?" Some among them had noticed the direction in which Christ and His disciples had gone. Many went by land to meet them, while others followed in their boats across the water. The Passover was at hand, and, from far and near, bands of pilgrims on their way to Jerusalem gathered to see Jesus. Additions were made to their number, until there were assembled five thousand men besides women and children. Before Christ reached the shore, a multitude were waiting for Him. But He landed unobserved by them, and spent a little time apart with the disciples.

From the hillside He looked upon the moving multitude, and His heart was stirred with sympathy. Interrupted as He was, and robbed of His rest, He was not impatient. He saw a greater necessity demanding His attention as He watched the people coming and still coming. He "was moved with compassion toward them, because they were as sheep not having a shepherd." Leaving His retreat, He found a convenient place where He could minister to them. They received no help from the priests and rulers; but the healing waters of life flowed from Christ as He taught the multitude the way of salvation.

The people listened to the words of mercy flowing so freely from the lips of the Son of God. They heard the gracious words, so simple and so plain that they were as the balm of Gilead to their souls. The healing of His divine hand brought gladness and life to the dying, and ease and health to those suffering with disease. The day seemed to them like heaven upon earth, and they were utterly unconscious of how long it had been since they had eaten anything.

At length the day was far spent. The sun was sinking in the west, and yet the people lingered. Jesus had labored all day without food or rest. He was pale from weariness and hunger, and the disciples besought Him to cease from His toil. But He could not withdraw Himself from the multitude that pressed upon Him.

The disciples finally came to Him, urging that for their own sake the people should be sent away. Many had come from far, and had eaten nothing since morning. In the surrounding towns and villages they might be able to buy food. But Jesus said, "Give ye them to eat," and then, turning to Philip, questioned, "Whence shall we buy bread, that these may eat?" This He said to test the faith of the disciple. Philip looked over the sea of heads, and thought how impossible it would be to provide food to satisfy the wants of such a crowd. He answered that two hundred pennyworth of bread would not be nearly enough to divide among them, so that each might have a little. Jesus inquired how much food could be found among the company. "There is a lad here," said Andrew, "which hath five barley loaves, and two small fishes; but what are they among so many?" Jesus directed that these be brought to Him. Then He bade the disciples seat the people on the grass in parties of fifty or a hundred, to preserve order, and that all might witness what He was about to do. When this was accomplished, Jesus took the food, "and looking up to heaven, He blessed, and brake, and gave the loaves to His disciples, and the disciples to the multitude." "And they did all eat, and were filled. And they took up twelve baskets full of the fragments, and of the fishes."

He who taught the people the way to secure peace and happiness was just as thoughtful of their temporal necessities as of their spiritual need. The people were weary and faint. There were mothers with babes in their arms, and little children clinging to their skirts. Many had been standing for hours. They had been so intensely interested in Christ's words that they had not once thought of sitting down, and the crowd was so great that there was danger of their trampling on one another. Jesus would give them a chance to rest, and He bade them sit down. There was much grass in the place, and all could rest in comfort.

Christ never worked a miracle except to supply a genuine necessity, and every miracle was of a character to lead the people to the tree of life, whose leaves are for the healing of the nations. The simple food passed round by the hands of the disciples contained a whole treasure of lessons. It was humble fare that had been provided; the fishes and barley loaves were the daily food of the fisher folk about the Sea of Galilee. Christ could have spread before the people a rich repast, but food prepared merely for the gratification of appetite would have conveyed no lesson for their good. Christ taught them in this lesson that the natural provisions of God for man had been perverted. And never did people enjoy the luxurious feasts prepared for the gratification of perverted taste as this people enjoyed the rest and the simple food which Christ provided so far from human habitations.

If men today were simple in their habits, living in harmony with nature's laws, as did Adam and Eve in the beginning, there would be an abundant supply for the needs of the human family. There would be fewer imaginary wants, and more opportunities to work in God's ways. But selfishness and the indulgence of unnatural taste have brought sin and misery into the world, from excess on the one hand, and from want on the other.

Jesus did not seek to attract the people to Him by gratifying the desire for luxury. To that great throng, weary and hungry after the long, exciting day, the simple fare was an assurance not only of His power, but of His tender care for them in the common needs of life. The Saviour has not promised His followers the luxuries of the world; their fare may be plain, and even scanty; their lot may be shut in by poverty; but His word is pledged that their need shall be supplied, and He has promised that which is far better than worldly good,—the abiding comfort of His own presence.

In feeding the five thousand, Jesus lifts the veil from the world of nature, and reveals the power that is constantly exercised for our good. In the production of earth's harvests God is working a miracle every day. Through natural agencies the same work is accomplished that was wrought in the feeding of the multitude. Men prepare the soil and sow the seed, but it is the life from God that causes the seed to germinate. It is God's rain and air and sunshine that cause it to put forth, "first the blade, then the ear, after that the full corn in the ear." Mark 4:28. It is God who is every day feeding millions from earth's harvest fields. Men are called upon to co-operate with God in the care of the grain and the preparation of the loaf, and because of this they lose sight of the divine agency. They do not give God the glory due unto His holy name. The working of His power is ascribed to natural causes or to human instrumentality. Man is glorified in place of God, and His gracious gifts are perverted to selfish uses, and made a curse instead of a blessing. God is seeking to change all this. He desires that our dull senses shall be quickened to discern His merciful kindness and to glorify Him for the working of His power. He desires us to recognize Him in His gifts, that they may be, as He intended, a blessing to us. It was to accomplish this purpose that the miracles of Christ were performed.

After the multitude had been fed, there was an abundance of food left. But He who had all the resources of infinite power at His command said, "Gather up the fragments that remain, that nothing be lost." These words meant more than putting the bread into the baskets. The lesson was twofold. Nothing is to be wasted. We are to let slip no temporal advantage. We should neglect nothing that will tend to benefit a human being. Let everything be gathered up that will relieve the necessity of earth's hungry ones. And there should be the same carefulness in spiritual things. When the baskets of fragments were collected, the people thought of their friends at home. They wanted them to share in the bread that Christ had blessed. The contents of the baskets were distributed among the eager throng, and were carried away into all the region round about. So those who were at the feast were to give to others the bread that comes down from heaven, to satisfy the hunger of the soul. They were to repeat what they had learned of the wonderful things of God. Nothing was to be lost. Not one word that concerned their eternal salvation was to fall useless to the ground.

The miracle of the loaves teaches a lesson of dependence upon God. When Christ fed the five thousand, the food was not nigh at hand. Apparently He had no means at His command. Here He was, with five thousand men, besides women and children, in the wilderness. He had not invited the large multitude to follow Him; they came without invitation or command; but He knew that after they had listened so long to His instruction, they would feel hungry and faint; for He was one with them in their need of food. They were far from home, and the night was close at hand. Many of them were without means to purchase food. He who for their sake had fasted forty days in the wilderness would not suffer them to return fasting to their homes. The providence of God had placed Jesus where He was; and He depended on His heavenly Father for the means to relieve the necessity.

And when we are brought into strait places, we are to depend on God. We are to exercise wisdom and judgment in every action of life, that we may not, by reckless movements, place ourselves in trial. We are not to plunge into difficulties, neglecting the means God has provided, and misusing the faculties He has given us. Christ's workers are to obey His instructions implicitly. The work is God's, and if we would bless others His plans must be followed. Self cannot be made a center; self can receive no honor. If we plan according to our own ideas, the Lord will leave us to our own mistakes. But when, after following His directions, we are brought into strait places, He will deliver us. We are not to give up in discouragement, but in every emergency we are to seek help from Him who has infinite resources at His command. Often we shall be surrounded with trying circumstances, and then, in the fullest confidence, we must depend upon God. He will keep every soul that is brought into perplexity through trying to keep the way of the Lord.

Christ has bidden us, through the prophet, "Deal thy bread to the hungry," and "satisfy the afflicted soul;" "when thou seest the naked, that thou cover him," and "bring the poor that are cast out to thy house." Isa. 58:7-10. He has bidden us, "Go ye into all the world, and preach the gospel to every creature." Mark 16:15. But how often our hearts sink, and faith fails us, as we see how great is the need, and how small the means in our hands. Like Andrew looking upon the five barley loaves and the two little fishes, we exclaim, "What are they among so many?" Often we hesitate, unwilling to give all that we have, fearing to spend and to be spent for others. But Jesus has bidden us, "Give *ye* them to eat." His command is a promise; and behind it is the same power that fed the multitude beside the sea.

In Christ's act of supplying the temporal necessities of a hungry multitude is wrapped up a deep spiritual lesson for all His workers. Christ received from the Father; He imparted to the disciples; they imparted to the multitude; and the people to one another. So all who are united to Christ will receive from Him the bread of life, the heavenly food, and impart it to others.

In full reliance upon God, Jesus took the small store of loaves; and although there was but a small portion for His own family of disciples, He did not invite them to eat, but began to distribute to them, bidding them serve the people. The food multiplied in His hands; and the hands of the disciples, reaching out to Christ Himself the Bread of Life, were never empty. The little store was sufficient for all. After the wants of the people had been supplied, the fragments were gathered up, and Christ and His disciples ate together of the precious, Heaven-supplied food.

The disciples were the channel of communication between Christ and the people. This should be a great encouragement to His disciples today. Christ is the great center, the source of all strength. His disciples are to receive their supplies from Him. The most intelligent, the most spiritually minded, can bestow only as they receive. Of themselves they can supply nothing for the needs of the soul. We can impart only that which we receive from Christ; and we can receive only as we impart to others. As we continue imparting, we continue to receive; and the more we impart, the more we shall receive. Thus we may be constantly believing, trusting, receiving, and imparting.

The work of building up the kingdom of Christ will go forward, though to all appearance it moves slowly and impossibilities seem to testify against advance. The work is of God, and He will furnish means, and will send helpers, true, earnest disciples, whose hands also will be filled with food for the starving multitude. God is not unmindful of those who labor in love to give the word of life to perishing souls, who in their turn reach forth their hands for food for other hungry souls.

In our work for God there is danger of relying too largely upon what man with his talents and ability can do. Thus we lose sight of the one Master Worker. Too often the worker for Christ fails to realize his personal responsibility. He is in danger of shifting his burden upon organizations, instead of relying upon Him who is the source of all strength. It is a great mistake to trust in human wisdom or numbers in the work of God. Successful work for Christ depends not so much on numbers or talent as upon pureness of purpose, the true simplicity of earnest, dependent faith. Personal responsibilities must be borne, personal duties must be taken up, personal efforts must be made for those who do not know Christ. In the place of shifting your responsibility upon someone whom you think more richly endowed than you are, work according to your ability.

When the question comes home to your heart, "Whence shall we buy bread, that these may eat?" let not your answer be the response of unbelief. When the disciples heard the Saviour's direction, "Give ye them to eat," all the difficulties arose in their minds. They questioned, Shall we go away into the villages to buy food? So now, when the people are destitute of the bread of life, the Lord's children question, Shall we send for someone from afar, to come and feed them? But what said Christ? "Make the men sit down," and He fed them there. So when you are surrounded by souls in need, know that Christ is there. Commune with Him. Bring your barley loaves to Jesus.

The means in our possession may not seem to be sufficient for the work; but if we will move forward in faith, believing in the all-sufficient power of God, abundant resources will open before us. If the work be of God, He Himself will provide the means for its accomplishment. He will reward honest, simple reliance upon Him. The little that is wisely and economically used in the service of the Lord of heaven will increase in the very act of imparting. In the hand of Christ the small supply of food remained undiminished until the famished multitude were satisfied. If we go to the Source of all strength, with our hands of faith outstretched to receive, we shall be sustained in our work, even under the most forbidding circumstances, and shall be enabled to give to others the bread of life.

The Lord says, "Give, and it shall be given unto you." "He that soweth sparingly shall reap also sparingly; and he that soweth with blessings shall reap also with blessings. . . . And God is able to make all grace abound unto you; that ye, having always all sufficiency in everything, may abound unto every good work; as it is written,—

"He hath scattered abroad, he hath given to the poor:
His righteousness abideth forever.

"And He that supplieth seed to the sower and bread for food, shall supply and multiply your seed for sowing, and increase the fruits of your righteousness: ye being enriched in everything unto all liberality, which worketh through us thanksgiving to God." Luke 6:38; 2 Cor. 9:6-11, R. V., margin.

2

A Night on the Lake

This chapter is based on Matthew 14:22-33; Mark 6:45-52; John 6:14-21.

S eated upon the grassy plain, in the twilight of the spring evening, the people ate of the food that Christ had provided. The words they had heard that day had come to them as the voice of God. The works of healing they had witnessed were such as only divine power could perform. But the miracle of the loaves appealed to everyone in that vast multitude. All were sharers in its benefit. In the days of Moses, God had fed Israel with manna in the desert; and who was this that had fed them that day but He whom Moses had foretold? No human power could create from five barley loaves and two small fishes food sufficient to feed thousands of hungry people. And they said one to another, "This is of a truth that Prophet that should come into the world."

All day the conviction has strengthened. That crowning act is assurance that the long-looked-for Deliverer is among them. The hopes of the people rise higher and higher. This is He who will make Judea an earthly paradise, a land flowing with milk and honey. He can satisfy every desire. He can break the power of the hated Romans. He can deliver Judah and Jerusalem. He can heal the soldiers who are wounded in battle. He can supply whole armies with food. He can conquer the nations, and give to Israel the long-sought dominion.

In their enthusiasm the people are ready at once to crown Him king. They see that He makes no effort to attract attention or secure honor to Himself. In this He is essentially different from the priests and rulers, and they fear that He will never urge His claim to David's throne. Consulting together, they agree to take Him by force, and proclaim Him the king of Israel. The disciples unite with the multitude in declaring the throne of David the rightful inheritance of their Master. It is the modesty of Christ, they say, that causes Him to refuse such honor. Let the people exalt their Deliverer. Let the arrogant priests and rulers be forced to honor Him who comes clothed with the authority of God.

They eagerly arrange to carry out their purpose; but Jesus sees what is on foot, and understands, as they cannot, what would be the result of such a movement. Even now the priests and rulers are hunting His life. They accuse Him of drawing the people away from them. Violence and insurrection would follow an effort to place Him on the throne, and the work of the spiritual kingdom would be hindered. Without delay the movement must be checked. Calling His disciples, Jesus bids them take the boat and return at once to Capernaum, leaving Him to dismiss the people.

Never before had a command from Christ seemed so impossible of fulfillment. The disciples had long hoped for a popular movement to place Jesus on the throne; they could not endure the thought that all this enthusiasm should come to nothing. The multitudes that were assembling to keep the Passover were anxious to see the new prophet. To His followers this seemed the golden opportunity to establish their beloved Master on the throne of Israel. In the glow of this new ambition it was hard for them to go away by themselves, and leave Jesus alone upon that desolate shore. They protested against the arrangement; but Jesus now spoke with an authority He had never before assumed toward them. They knew that further opposition on their part would be useless, and in silence they turned toward the sea.

Jesus now commands the multitude to disperse; and His manner is so decisive that they dare not disobey. The words of praise and exaltation die on their lips. In the very act of advancing to seize Him their steps are stayed, and the glad, eager look fades from their countenances. In that throng are men of strong mind and firm determination; but the kingly bearing of Jesus, and His few quiet words of command, quell the tumult, and frustrate their designs. They recognize in Him a power above all earthly authority, and without a question they submit.

When left alone, Jesus "went up into a mountain apart to pray." For hours He continued pleading with God. Not for Himself but for men were those prayers. He prayed for power to reveal to men the divine character of His mission, that Satan might not blind their understanding and pervert their judgment. The Saviour knew that His days of personal ministry on earth were nearly ended, and that few would receive Him as their Redeemer. In travail and conflict of soul He prayed for His disciples. They were to be grievously tried. Their long-cherished hopes, based on a popular delusion, were to be disappointed in a most painful and humiliating manner. In the place of His exaltation to the throne of David they were to witness His crucifixion. This was to be indeed His true coronation. But they did not discern this, and in consequence strong temptations would come to them, which it would be difficult for them to recognize as temptations. Without the Holy Spirit to enlighten the mind and enlarge the comprehension the faith of the disciples would fail. It was painful to Jesus that their conceptions of His kingdom were, to so great a degree, limited to worldly aggrandizement and honor. For them the burden was heavy upon His heart, and He poured out His supplications with bitter agony and tears.

The disciples had not put off immediately from the land, as Jesus directed them. They waited for a time, hoping that He would come to them. But as they saw that darkness was fast gathering, they "entered into a ship, and went over the sea toward Capernaum." They had left Jesus with dissatisfied hearts, more impatient with Him than ever before since acknowledging Him as their Lord. They murmured because they had not been permitted to proclaim Him king. They blamed themselves for yielding so readily to His command. They reasoned that if they had been more persistent they might have accomplished their purpose.

Unbelief was taking possession of their minds and hearts. Love of honor had blinded them. They knew that Jesus was hated by the Pharisees, and they were eager to see Him exalted as they thought He should be. To be united with a teacher who could work mighty miracles, and yet to be reviled as deceivers, was a trial they could ill endure. Were they always to be accounted followers of a false prophet? Would Christ never assert His authority as king? Why did not He who possessed such power reveal Himself in His true character, and make their way less painful? Why had He not saved John the Baptist from a violent death? Thus the disciples reasoned until they brought upon themselves great spiritual darkness. They questioned, Could Jesus be an impostor, as the Pharisees asserted?

The disciples had that day witnessed the wonderful works of Christ. It had seemed that heaven had come down to the earth. The memory of that precious, glorious day should have filled them with faith and hope. Had they, out of the abundance of their hearts, been conversing together in regard to these things, they would not have entered into temptation. But their disappointment had absorbed their thoughts. The words of Christ, "Gather up the fragments, . . . that nothing be lost," were unheeded. Those were hours of large blessing to the disciples, but they had forgotten it all. They were in the midst of troubled waters. Their thoughts were stormy and unreasonable, and the Lord gave them something else to afflict their souls and occupy their minds. God often does this when men create burdens and troubles for themselves. The disciples had no need to make trouble. Already danger was fast approaching.

A violent tempest had been stealing upon them, and they were unprepared for it. It was a sudden contrast, for the day had been perfect; and when the gale struck them, they were afraid. They forgot their disaffection, their unbelief, their impatience. Everyone worked to keep the boat from sinking. It was but a short distance by sea from Bethsaida to the point where they expected to meet Jesus, and in ordinary weather the journey required but a few hours; but now they were driven farther and farther from the point they sought. Until the fourth watch of the night they toiled at the oars. Then the weary men gave themselves up for lost. In storm and darkness the sea had taught them their own helplessness, and they longed for the presence of their Master.

Jesus had not forgotten them. The Watcher on the shore saw those fear-stricken men battling with the tempest. Not for a moment did He lose sight of His disciples. With deepest solicitude His eyes followed the storm-tossed boat with its precious burden; for these men were to be the light of the world. As a mother in tender love watches her child, so the compassionate Master watched His disciples. When their hearts were subdued, their unholy ambition quelled, and in humility they prayed for help, it was given them.

At the moment when they believe themselves lost, a gleam of light reveals a mysterious figure approaching them upon the water. But they know not that it is Jesus. The One who has come for their help they count as an enemy. Terror overpowers them. The hands that have grasped the oars with muscles like iron let go their hold. The boat rocks at the will of the waves; all eyes are riveted on this vision of a man walking upon the white-capped billows of the foaming sea.

They think it a phantom that omens their destruction, and they cry out for fear. Jesus advances as if He would pass them; but they recognize Him, and cry out, entreating His help. Their beloved Master turns, His voice silences their fear, "Be of good cheer: it is I; be not afraid."

As soon as they could credit the wondrous fact, Peter was almost beside himself with joy. As if he could scarcely yet believe, he cried out, "Lord, if it be Thou, bid me come unto Thee on the water. And He said, Come."

Looking unto Jesus, Peter walks securely; but as in self-satisfaction he glances back toward his companions in the boat, his eyes are turned from the Saviour. The wind is boisterous. The waves roll high, and come directly between him and the Master; and he is afraid. For a moment Christ is hidden from his view, and his faith gives way. He begins to sink. But while the billows talk with death, Peter lifts his eyes from the angry waters, and fixing them upon Jesus, cries, "Lord, save me." Immediately Jesus grasps the outstretched hand, saying, "O thou of little faith, wherefore didst thou doubt?"

Walking side by side, Peter's hand in that of his Master, they stepped into the boat together. But Peter was now subdued and silent. He had no reason to boast over his fellows, for through unbelief and self-exaltation he had very nearly lost his life. When he turned his eyes from Jesus, his footing was lost, and he sank amid the waves.

When trouble comes upon us, how often we are like Peter! We look upon the waves, instead of keeping our eyes fixed upon the Saviour. Our footsteps slide, and the proud waters go over our souls. Jesus did not bid Peter come to Him that he should perish; He does not call us to follow Him, and then forsake us. "Fear not," He says; "for I have redeemed thee, I have called thee by thy name; thou art Mine. When thou passest through the waters, I will be with thee; and through the rivers, they shall not overflow thee: when thou walkest through the fire, thou shalt not be burned; neither shall the flame kindle upon thee. For I am the Lord thy God, the Holy One of Israel, thy Saviour." Isa. 43:1-3.

Jesus read the character of His disciples. He knew how sorely their faith was to be tried. In this incident on the sea He desired to reveal to Peter his own weakness,—to show that his safety was in constant dependence upon divine power. Amid the storms of temptation he could walk safely only as in utter self-distrust he should rely upon the Saviour. It was on the point where he thought himself strong that Peter was weak; and not until he discerned his weakness could he realize his need of dependence upon Christ. Had he learned the lesson that Jesus sought to teach him in that experience on the sea, he would not have failed when the great test came upon him.

Day by day God instructs His children. By the circumstances of the daily life He is preparing them to act their part upon that wider stage to which His providence has appointed them. It is the issue of the daily test that determines their victory or defeat in life's great crisis.

Those who fail to realize their constant dependence upon God will be overcome by temptation. We may now suppose that our feet stand secure, and that we shall never be moved. We may say with confidence, "I know in whom I have believed; nothing can shake my faith in God and in His word." But Satan is planning to take advantage of our hereditary and cultivated traits of character, and to blind our eyes to our own necessities and defects. Only through realizing our own weakness and looking steadfastly unto Jesus can we walk securely.

No sooner had Jesus taken His place in the boat than the wind ceased, "and immediately the ship was at the land whither they went." The night of horror was succeeded by the light of dawn. The disciples, and others who also were on board, bowed at the feet of Jesus with thankful hearts, saying, "Of a truth Thou art the Son of God!"

3

The Crisis in Galilee

This chapter is based on John 6:22-71.

W hen Christ forbade the people to declare Him king, He knew that a turning point in His history was reached. Multitudes who desired to exalt Him to the throne today would turn from Him tomorrow. The disappointment of their selfish ambition would turn their love to hatred, and their praise to curses. Yet knowing this, He took no measures to avert the crisis. From the first He had held out to His followers no hope of earthly rewards. To one who came desiring to become His disciple He had said, "The foxes have holes, and the birds of the air have nests; but the Son of man hath not where to lay His head." Matt. 8:20. If men could have had the world with Christ, multitudes would have proffered Him their allegiance; but such service He could not accept. Of those now connected with Him there were many who had been attracted by the hope of a worldly kingdom. These must be undeceived. The deep spiritual teaching in the miracle of the loaves had not been comprehended. This was to be made plain. And this new revelation would bring with it a closer test.

The miracle of the loaves was reported far and near, and very early next morning the people flocked to Bethsaida to see Jesus. They came in great numbers, by land and sea. Those who had left Him the preceding night returned, expecting to find Him still there; for there had been no boat by which He could pass to the other side. But their search was fruitless, and many repaired to Capernaum, still seeking Him.

Meanwhile He had arrived at Gennesaret, after an absence of but one day. As soon as it was known that He had landed, the people "ran through that whole region round about, and began to carry about in beds those that were sick, where they heard He was." Mark 6:55.

After a time He went to the synagogue, and there those who had come from Bethsaida found Him. They learned from His disciples how He had crossed the sea. The fury of the storm, and the many hours of fruitless rowing against adverse winds, the appearance of Christ walking upon the water, the fears thus aroused, His reassuring words, the adventure of Peter and its result, with the sudden stilling of the tempest and landing of the boat, were all faithfully recounted to the wondering crowd. Not content with this, however, many gathered about Jesus, questioning, "Rabbi, when camest Thou hither?" They hoped to receive from His own lips a further account of the miracle.

Jesus did not gratify their curiosity. He sadly said, "Ye seek Me, not because ye saw the miracles, but because ye did eat of the loaves, and were filled." They did not seek Him from any worthy motive; but as they had been fed with the loaves, they hoped still to receive temporal benefit by attaching themselves to Him. The Saviour bade them, "Labor not for the meat which perisheth, but for that meat which endureth unto everlasting life." Seek not merely for material benefit. Let it not be the chief effort to provide for the life that now is, but seek for spiritual food, even that wisdom which will endure unto everlasting life. This the Son of God alone can give; "for Him hath God the Father sealed."

For the moment the interest of the hearers was awakened. They exclaimed, "What shall we do, that we might work the works of God?" They had been performing many and burdensome works in order to recommend themselves to God; and they were ready to hear of any new observance by which they could secure greater merit. Their question meant, What shall we do that we may deserve heaven? What is the price we are required to pay in order to obtain the life to come?

"Jesus answered and said unto them, This is the work of God, that ye believe on Him whom He hath sent." The price of heaven is Jesus. The way to heaven is through faith in "the Lamb of God, which taketh away the sin of the world." John 1:29.

But the people did not choose to receive this statement of divine truth. Jesus had done the very work which prophecy had foretold that the Messiah would do; but they had not witnessed what their selfish hopes had pictured as His work. Christ had indeed once fed the multitude with barley loaves; but in the days of Moses Israel had been fed with manna forty years, and far greater blessings were expected from the Messiah. Their dissatisfied hearts queried why, if Jesus could perform so many wondrous works as they had witnessed, could He not give health, strength, and riches to all His people, free them from their oppressors, and exalt them to power and honor? The fact that He claimed to be the Sent of God, and yet refused to be Israel's king, was a mystery which they could not fathom. His refusal was misinterpreted. Many concluded that He dared not assert His claims because He Himself doubted as to the divine character of His mission. Thus they opened their hearts to unbelief, and the seed which Satan had sown bore fruit of its kind, in misunderstanding and defection.

Now, half mockingly, a rabbi questioned, "What sign showest Thou then, that we may see, and believe Thee? what dost Thou work? Our fathers did eat manna in the desert; as it is written, He gave them bread from heaven to eat."

The Jews honored Moses as the giver of the manna, ascribing praise to the instrument, and losing sight of Him by whom the work had been accomplished. Their fathers had murmured against Moses, and had doubted and denied his divine mission. Now in the same spirit the children rejected the One who bore the message of God to themselves. "Then said Jesus unto them, Verily, verily, I say unto you, Moses gave you not that bread from heaven." The giver of the manna was standing among them. It was Christ Himself who had led the Hebrews through the wilderness, and had daily fed them with the bread from heaven. That food was a type of the real bread from heaven. The life-giving Spirit, flowing from the infinite fullness of God, is the true manna. Jesus said, "The bread of God is that which cometh down out of heaven, and giveth life unto the world." John 6:33, R. V.

Still thinking that it was temporal food to which Jesus referred, some of His hearers exclaimed, "Lord, evermore give us this bread." Jesus then spoke plainly: "I am the bread of life."

The figure which Christ used was a familiar one to the Jews. Moses, by the inspiration of the Holy Spirit, had said, "Man doth not live by bread only, but by every word that proceedeth out of the mouth of the Lord." And the prophet Jeremiah had written, "Thy words were found, and I did eat them; and Thy word was unto me the joy and rejoicing of mine heart." Deut. 8:3; Jer. 15:16. The rabbis themselves had a saying, that the eating of bread, in its spiritual significance, was the study of the law and the practice of good works; and it was often said that at the Messiah's coming all Israel would be fed. The teaching of the prophets made plain the deep spiritual lesson in the miracle of the loaves. This lesson Christ was seeking to open to His hearers in the synagogue. Had they understood the Scriptures, they would have understood His words when He said, "I am the bread of life." Only the day before, the great multitude, when faint and weary, had been fed by the bread which He had given. As from that bread they had received physical strength and refreshment, so from Christ they might receive spiritual strength unto eternal life. "He that cometh to Me," He said, "shall never hunger; and he that believeth on Me shall never thirst." But He added, "Ye also have seen Me, and believe not."

They had seen Christ by the witness of the Holy Spirit, by the revelation of God to their souls. The living evidences of His power had been before them day after day, yet they asked for still another sign. Had this been given, they would have remained as unbelieving as before. If they were not convinced by what they had seen and heard, it was useless to show them more marvelous works. Unbelief will ever find excuse for doubt, and will reason away the most positive proof.

Again Christ appealed to those stubborn hearts. "Him that cometh to Me I will in nowise cast out." All who received Him in faith, He said, should have eternal life. Not one could be lost. No need for Pharisees and Sadducees to dispute concerning the future life. No longer need men mourn in hopeless grief over their dead. "This is the will of Him that sent Me, that everyone which seeth the

Son, and believeth on Him, may have everlasting life: and I will raise him up at the last day."

But the leaders of the people were offended, "and they said, Is not this Jesus, the son of Joseph, whose father and mother we know? how is it then that He saith, I came down from heaven?" They tried to arouse prejudice by referring scornfully to the lowly origin of Jesus. They contemptuously alluded to His life as a Galilean laborer, and to His family as being poor and lowly. The claims of this uneducated carpenter, they said, were unworthy of their attention. And on account of His mysterious birth they insinuated that He was of doubtful parentage, thus representing the human circumstances of His birth as a blot upon His history.

Jesus did not attempt to explain the mystery of His birth. He made no answer to the questionings in regard to His having come down from heaven, as He had made none to the questions concerning His crossing the sea. He did not call attention to the miracles that marked His life. Voluntarily He had made Himself of no reputation, and taken upon Him the form of a servant. But His words and works revealed His character. All whose hearts were open to divine illumination would recognize in Him "the Only-begotten of the Father, full of grace and truth." John 1:14.

The prejudice of the Pharisees lay deeper than their questions would indicate; it had its root in the perversity of their hearts. Every word and act of Jesus aroused antagonism in them; for the spirit which they cherished could find in Him no answering chord.

"No man can come to Me, except the Father which hath sent Me draw him: and I will raise him up at the last day. It is written in the prophets, And they shall be all taught of God. Every man therefore that hath heard, and hath learned of the Father, cometh unto Me." None will ever come to Christ, save those who respond to the drawing of the Father's love. But God is drawing all hearts unto Him, and only those who resist His drawing will refuse to come to Christ.

In the words, "They shall be all taught of God," Jesus referred to the prophecy of Isaiah: "All thy children shall be taught of the Lord; and great shall be the peace of thy children." Isa. 54:13. This scripture the Jews appropriated to themselves. It was their boast that God was their teacher. But Jesus showed how vain is this claim; for He said, "Every man therefore that hath heard, and hath learned of the Father, cometh unto Me." Only through Christ could they receive a knowledge of the Father. Humanity could not endure the vision of His glory. Those who had learned of God had been listening to the voice of His Son, and in Jesus of Nazareth they would recognize Him who through nature and revelation has declared the Father.

"Verily, verily, I say unto you, He that believeth on Me hath everlasting life." Through the beloved John, who listened to these words, the Holy Spirit declared to the churches, "This is the record, that God hath given to us eternal life, and this life is in His Son. He that hath the Son hath life." 1 John 5:11, 12. And Jesus said, "I will raise him up at the last day." Christ became one flesh with us, in order that we might become one spirit with Him. It is by virtue of this union that we are to come forth from the grave,—not merely as a manifestation of the power of Christ, but because, through faith, His life has become ours. Those who see Christ in His true character, and receive Him into the heart, have everlasting life. It is through the Spirit that Christ dwells in us; and the Spirit of God, received into the heart by faith, is the beginning of the life eternal.

The people had referred Christ to the manna which their fathers ate in the wilderness, as if the furnishing of that food was a greater miracle than Jesus had performed; but He shows how meager was that gift when compared with the blessings He had come to bestow. The manna could sustain only this earthly existence; it did not prevent the approach of death, nor insure immortality; but the bread of heaven would nourish the soul unto everlasting life. The Saviour said, "I am that bread of life. Your fathers did eat manna in the wilderness, and are dead. This is the bread which cometh down from heaven, that a man may eat thereof, and not die. I am the living bread which came down from heaven: if any man eat of this bread, he shall live forever." To this figure Christ now adds another. Only through dying could He impart life to men, and in the words that follow He points to His death as the means of salvation. He says, "The bread that I will give is My flesh, which I will give for the life of the world."

The Jews were about to celebrate the Passover at Jerusalem, in commemoration of the night of Israel's deliverance, when the destroying angel smote the homes of Egypt. In the paschal lamb God desired them to behold the Lamb of God, and through the symbol receive Him who gave Himself for the life of the world. But the Jews had come to make the symbol all-important, while its significance was unnoticed. They discerned not the Lord's body. The same truth that was symbolized in the paschal service was taught in the words of Christ. But it was still undiscerned.

Now the rabbis exclaimed angrily, "How can this Man give us His flesh to eat?" They affected to understand His words in the same literal sense as did Nicodemus when he asked, "How can a man be born when he is old?" John 3:4. To some extent they comprehended the meaning of Jesus, but they were not willing to acknowledge it. By misconstruing His words, they hoped to prejudice the people against Him.

Christ did not soften down His symbolical representation. He reiterated the truth in yet stronger language: "Verily, verily, I say unto you, Except ye eat the flesh of the Son of man, and drink His blood, ye have no life in you. Whoso eateth My flesh, and drinketh My blood, hath eternal life; and I will raise him up at the last day. For My flesh is meat indeed, and My blood is drink indeed. He that eateth My flesh, and drinketh My blood, dwelleth in Me, and I in him."

To eat the flesh and drink the blood of Christ is to receive Him as a personal Saviour, believing that He forgives our sins, and that we are complete in Him. It is by beholding His love, by dwelling upon it, by drinking it in, that we are to become partakers of His nature. What food is to the body, Christ must be to the soul. Food cannot benefit us unless we eat it, unless it becomes a part of our being. So Christ is of no value to us if we do not know Him as a personal Saviour. A theoretical knowledge will do us no good. We must feed upon Him, receive Him into the heart, so that His life becomes our life. His love, His grace, must be assimilated.

But even these figures fail to present the privilege of the believer's relation to Christ. Jesus said, "As the living Father hath sent Me, and I live by the Father: so he that eateth Me, even he shall live by Me." As the Son of God lived by faith in the Father, so are we to live by faith in Christ. So fully was Jesus surrendered to the will of

God that the Father alone appeared in His life. Although tempted in all points like as we are, He stood before the world untainted by the evil that surrounded Him. Thus we also are to overcome as Christ overcame.

Are you a follower of Christ? Then all that is written concerning the spiritual life is written for you, and may be attained through uniting yourself to Jesus. Is your zeal languishing? has your first love grown cold? Accept again of the proffered love of Christ. Eat of His flesh, drink of His blood, and you will become one with the Father and with the Son.

The unbelieving Jews refused to see any except the most literal meaning in the Saviour's words. By the ritual law they were forbidden to taste blood, and they now construed Christ's language into a sacrilegious speech, and disputed over it among themselves. Many even of the disciples said, "This is an hard saying; who can hear it?"

The Saviour answered them: "Doth *this* offend you? What and if ye shall see the Son of man ascend up where He was before? It is the spirit that quickeneth; the flesh profiteth nothing: the words that I speak unto you, they are spirit, and they are life."

The life of Christ that gives life to the world is in His word. It was by His word that Jesus healed disease and cast out demons; by His word He stilled the sea, and raised the dead; and the people bore witness that His word was with power. He spoke the word of God, as He had spoken through all the prophets and teachers of the Old Testament. The whole Bible is a manifestation of Christ, and the Saviour desired to fix the faith of His followers on the word. When His visible presence should be withdrawn, the word must be their source of power. Like their Master, they were to live "by every word that proceedeth out of the mouth of God." Matt. 4:4.

As our physical life is sustained by food, so our spiritual life is sustained by the word of God. And every soul is to receive life from God's word for himself. As we must eat for ourselves in order to receive nourishment, so we must receive the word for ourselves. We are not to obtain it merely through the medium of another's mind. We should carefully study the Bible, asking God for the aid of the Holy Spirit, that we may understand His word. We should take one verse, and concentrate the mind on the task of ascertaining the thought which God has put in that verse for us. We should dwell upon the thought until it becomes our own, and we know "what saith the Lord."

In His promises and warnings, Jesus means me. God so loved the world, that He gave His only-begotten Son, that *I* by believing in Him, might not perish, but have everlasting life. The experiences related in God's word are to be *my* experiences. Prayer and promise, precept and warning, are mine. "I am crucified with Christ: nevertheless I live; yet not I, but Christ liveth in me: and the life which I now live in the flesh I live by the faith of the Son of God, who loved *me*, and gave Himself for *me*." Gal. 2:20. As faith thus receives and assimilates the principles of truth, they become a part of the being and the motive power of the life. The word of God, received into the soul, molds the thoughts, and enters into the development of character.

By looking constantly to Jesus with the eye of faith, we shall be strengthened. God will make the most precious revelations to His hungering, thirsting people. They will find that Christ is a personal Saviour. As they feed upon His word, they find that it is spirit and life. The word destroys the natural, earthly nature, and imparts a new life in Christ Jesus. The Holy Spirit comes to the soul as a Comforter. By the transforming agency of His grace, the image of God is reproduced in the disciple; he becomes a new creature. Love takes the place of hatred, and the heart receives the divine similitude. This is what it means to live "by every word that proceedeth out of the mouth of God." This is eating the Bread that comes down from heaven.

Christ had spoken a sacred, eternal truth regarding the relation between Himself and His followers. He knew the character of those who claimed to be His disciples, and His words tested their faith. He declared that they were to believe and act upon His teaching. All who received Him would partake of His nature, and be conformed to His character. This involved the relinquishment of their cherished ambitions. It required the complete surrender of themselves to Jesus. They were called to become self-sacrificing, meek and lowly in heart. They must walk in the narrow path traveled by the Man of Calvary, if they would share in the gift of life and the glory of heaven.

The test was too great. The enthusiasm of those who had sought to take Him by force and make Him king grew cold. This discourse in the synagogue, they declared, had opened their eyes. Now they were undeceived. In their minds His words were a direct confession that He was not the Messiah, and that no earthly rewards were to be realized from connection with Him. They had welcomed His miracle-working power; they were eager to be freed from disease and suffering; but they would not come into sympathy with His self-sacrificing life. They cared not for the mysterious spiritual kingdom of which He spoke. The insincere, the selfish, who had sought Him, no longer desired Him. If He would not devote His power and influence to obtaining their freedom from the Romans, they would have nothing to do with Him.

Jesus told them plainly, "There are some of you that believe not;" adding, "Therefore said I unto you, that no man can come unto Me, except it were given unto him of My Father." He wished them to understand that if they were not drawn to Him it was because their hearts were not open to the Holy Spirit. "The natural man receiveth not the things of the Spirit of God: for they are foolishness unto him: neither can he know them, because they are spiritually discerned." 1 Cor. 2:14. It is by faith that the soul beholds the glory of Jesus. This glory is hidden, until, through the Holy Spirit, faith is kindled in the soul.

By the public rebuke of their unbelief these disciples were still further alienated from Jesus. They were greatly displeased, and wishing to wound the Saviour and gratify the malice of the Pharisees, they turned their backs upon Him, and left Him with disdain. They had made their choice,—had taken the form without the spirit, the husk without the kernel. Their decision was never afterward reversed; for they walked no more with Jesus.

"Whose fan is in His hand, and He will throughly purge His floor, and gather His wheat into the garner." Matt. 3:12. This was one of the times of purging. By the words of truth, the chaff was being separated from the wheat. Because they were too vain and self-righteous to receive reproof, too world-loving to accept a life of humility, many turned away from Jesus. Many are still doing the same thing. Souls are tested today as were those disciples in the synagogue at Capernaum. When truth is brought home to the heart, they see that their lives are not in accordance with the will of God. They see the need of an entire change in themselves; but they are not willing to take up the self-denying work. Therefore they are angry when their sins are discovered. They go away offended, even as the disciples left Jesus, murmuring, "This is an hard saying; who can hear it?"

Praise and flattery would be pleasing to their ears; but the truth is unwelcome; they cannot hear it. When the crowds follow, and the multitudes are fed, and the shouts of triumph are heard, their voices are loud in praise; but when the searching of God's Spirit reveals their sin, and bids them leave it, they turn their backs upon the truth, and walk no more with Jesus.

As those disaffected disciples turned away from Christ, a different spirit took control of them. They could see nothing attractive in Him whom they had once found so interesting. They sought out His enemies, for they were in harmony with their spirit and work. They misinterpreted His words, falsified His statements, and impugned His motives. They sustained their course by gathering up every item that could be turned against Him; and such indignation was stirred up by these false reports that His life was in danger.

The news spread swiftly that by His own confession Jesus of Nazareth was not the Messiah. And thus in Galilee the current of popular feeling was turned against Him, as, the year before, it had been in Judea. Alas for Israel! They rejected their Saviour, because they longed for a conqueror who would give them temporal power. They wanted the meat which perishes, and not that which endures unto everlasting life.

With a yearning heart, Jesus saw those who had been His disciples departing from Him, the Life and the Light of men. The consciousness that His compassion was unappreciated, His love unrequited, His mercy slighted, His salvation rejected, filled Him with sorrow that was inexpressible. It was such developments as these that made Him a man of sorrows, and acquainted with grief.

Without attempting to hinder those who were leaving Him,

Jesus turned to the twelve and said, "Will ye also go away?"

Peter replied by asking, "Lord, to whom shall we go?" "Thou hast the words of eternal life," he added. "And we believe and are sure that Thou art that Christ, the Son of the living God."

"To whom shall we go?" The teachers of Israel were slaves to formalism. The Pharisees and Sadducees were in constant contention. To leave Jesus was to fall among sticklers for rites and ceremonies, and ambitious men who sought their own glory. The disciples had found more peace and joy since they had accepted Christ than in all their previous lives. How could they go back to those who had scorned and persecuted the Friend of sinners? They had long been looking for the Messiah; now He had come, and they could not turn from His presence to those who were hunting His life, and had persecuted them for becoming His followers.

"To whom shall we go?" Not from the teaching of Christ, His lessons of love and mercy, to the darkness of unbelief, the wickedness of the world. While the Saviour was forsaken by many who had witnessed His wonderful works, Peter expressed the faith of the disciples,—"Thou art that Christ." The very thought of losing this anchor of their souls filled them with fear and pain. To be destitute of a Saviour was to be adrift on a dark and stormy sea.

Many of the words and acts of Jesus appear mysterious to finite minds, but every word and act had its definite purpose in the work for our redemption; each was calculated to produce its own result. If we were capable of understanding His purposes, all would appear important, complete, and in harmony with His mission.

While we cannot now comprehend the works and ways of God, we can discern His great love, which underlies all His dealings with men. He who lives near to Jesus will understand much of the mystery of godliness. He will recognize the mercy that administers reproof, that tests the character, and brings to light the purpose of the heart.

When Jesus presented the testing truth that caused so many of His disciples to turn back, He knew what would be the result of His words; but He had a purpose of mercy to fulfill. He foresaw that in the hour of temptation every one of His beloved disciples would be severely tested. His agony in Gethsemane, His betrayal and crucifixion, would be to them a most trying ordeal. Had no previous test been given, many who were actuated by merely selfish motives would have been connected with them. When their Lord was condemned in the judgment hall; when the multitude who had hailed Him as their king hissed at Him and reviled Him; when the jeering crowd cried, "Crucify Him!"—when their worldly ambitions were disappointed, these self-seeking ones would, by renouncing their allegiance to Jesus, have brought upon the disciples a bitter, heart-burdening sorrow, in addition to their grief and disappointment in the ruin of their fondest hopes. In that hour of darkness, the example of those who turned from Him might have carried others with them. But Jesus brought about this crisis while by His personal presence He could still strengthen the faith of His true followers.

Compassionate Redeemer, who in the full knowledge of the doom that awaited Him, tenderly smoothed the way for the disciples, prepared them for their crowning trial, and strengthened them for the final test!

4

Tradition

This chapter is based on Matthew 15:1-20; Mark 7:1-23.

T he scribes and Pharisees, expecting to see Jesus at the Passover, had laid a trap for Him. But Jesus, knowing their purpose, had absented Himself from this gathering. "Then came together unto Him the Pharisees, and certain of the scribes." As He did not go to them, they came to Him. For a time it had seemed that the people of Galilee would receive Jesus as the Messiah, and that the power of the hierarchy in that region would be broken. The mission of the twelve, indicating the extension of Christ's work, and bringing the disciples more directly into conflict with the rabbis, had excited anew the jealousy of the leaders at Jerusalem. The spies they sent to Capernaum in the early part of His ministry, who had tried to fix on Him the charge of Sabbathbreaking, had been put to confusion; but the rabbis were bent on carrying out their purpose. Now another deputation was sent to watch His movements, and find some accusation against Him.

As before, the ground of complaint was His disregard of the traditional precepts that encumbered the law of God. These were professedly designed to guard the observance of the law, but they were regarded as more sacred than the law itself. When they came in collision with the commandments given from Sinai, preference was given to the rabbinical precepts.

Among the observances most strenuously enforced was that of ceremonial purification. A neglect of the forms to be observed before eating was accounted a heinous sin, to be punished both in this world and in the next; and it was regarded as a virtue to destroy the transgressor.

The rules in regard to purification were numberless. The period of a lifetime was scarcely sufficient for one to learn them all. The life of those who tried to observe the rabbinical requirements was one long struggle against ceremonial defilement, an endless round of washings and purifications. While the people were occupied with trifling distinctions, and observances which God had not required, their attention was turned away from the great principles of His law.

Christ and His disciples did not observe these ceremonial washings, and the spies made this neglect the ground of their accusation. They did not, however, make a direct attack on Christ, but came to Him with criticism of His disciples. In the presence of the multitude they said, "Why do Thy disciples transgress the tradition of the elders? for they wash not their hands when they eat bread."

Whenever the message of truth comes home to souls with special power, Satan stirs up his agents to start a dispute over some minor question. Thus he seeks to attract attention from the real issue. Whenever a good work is begun, there are cavilers ready to enter into dispute over forms or technicalities, to draw minds away from the living realities. When it appears that God is about to work in a special manner for His people, let them not be enticed into a controversy that will work only ruin of souls. The questions that most concern us are, Do I believe with saving faith on the Son of God? Is my life in harmony with the divine law? "He that believeth on the Son hath everlasting life: and he that believeth not the Son shall not see life." "And hereby we do know that we know Him, if we keep His commandments." John 3:36; 1 John 2:3.

Jesus made no attempt to defend Himself or His disciples. He made no reference to the charges against Him, but proceeded to show the spirit that actuated these sticklers for human rites. He gave them an example of what they were repeatedly doing, and had done just before coming in search of Him. "Full well ye reject the commandment of God," He said, "that ye may keep your own tradition. For Moses said, Honor thy father and thy mother; and, Whoso curseth father or mother, let him die the death: but ye say, If a man shall say to his father or mother, It is Corban, that is to say, a gift, by whatsoever thou mightest be profited by me; he shall be free. And ye suffer him no more to do aught for his father or his mother." They set aside the fifth commandment as of no consequence, but were very exact in carrying out the traditions of the elders. They taught the people that the devotion of their property to the temple was a duty more sacred than even the support of their parents; and that, however great the necessity, it was sacrilege to impart to father or mother any part of what had been thus consecrated. An undutiful child had only to pronounce the word "Corban" over his property, thus devoting it to God, and he could retain it for his own use during his lifetime, and after his death it was to be appropriated to the temple service. Thus he was at liberty, both in life and in death, to dishonor and defraud his parents, under cover of a pretended devotion to God.

Never, by word or deed, did Jesus lessen man's obligation to present gifts and offerings to God. It was Christ who gave all the directions of the law in regard to tithes and offerings. When on earth He commended the poor woman who gave her all to the temple treasury. But the apparent zeal for God on the part of the priests and rabbis was a pretense to cover their desire for self-aggrandizement. The people were deceived by them. They were bearing heavy burdens which God had not imposed. Even the disciples of Christ were not wholly free from the yoke that had been bound upon them by inherited prejudice and rabbinical authority. Now, by revealing the true spirit of the rabbis, Jesus sought to free from the bondage of tradition all who were really desirous of serving God.

"Ye hypocrites," He said, addressing the wily spies, "well did Esaias prophesy of you, saying, This people draweth nigh unto Me with their mouth, and honoreth Me with their lips; but their heart is far from Me. But in vain they do worship Me, teaching for doctrines the commandments of men." The words of Christ were an arraignment of the whole system of Pharisaism. He declared that by placing their requirements above the divine precepts the rabbis were setting themselves above God.

The deputies from Jerusalem were filled with rage. They could not accuse Christ as a violator of the law given from Sinai, for He spoke as its defender against their traditions. The great precepts of the law, which He had presented, appeared in striking contrast to the petty rules that men had devised.

To the multitude, and afterward more fully to His disciples, Jesus explained that defilement comes not from without, but from within. Purity and impurity pertain to the soul. It is the evil deed, the evil word, the evil thought, the transgression of the law of God, not the neglect of external, man-made ceremonies, that defiles a man.

The disciples noted the rage of the spies as their false teaching was exposed. They saw the angry looks, and heard the half-muttered words of dissatisfaction and revenge. Forgetting how often Christ had given evidence that He read the heart as an open book, they told Him of the effect of His words. Hoping that He might conciliate the enraged officials, they said to Jesus, "Knowest Thou that the Pharisees were offended, after they heard this saying?"

He answered, "Every plant, which My heavenly Father hath not planted, shall be rooted up." The customs and traditions so highly valued by the rabbis were of this world, not from heaven. However great their authority with the people, they could not endure the testing of God. Every human invention that has been substituted for the commandments of God will be found worthless in that day when "God shall bring every work into judgment, with every secret thing, whether it be good, or whether it be evil." Eccl. 12:14.

The substitution of the precepts of men for the commandments of God has not ceased. Even among Christians are found institutions and usages that have no better foundation than the traditions of the fathers. Such institutions, resting upon mere human authority, have supplanted those of divine appointment. Men cling to their traditions, and revere their customs, and cherish hatred against those who seek to show them their error. In this day, when we are bidden to call attention to the commandments of God and the faith of Jesus, we see the same enmity as was manifested in the days of Christ. Of the remnant people of God it is written, "The dragon was wroth with the woman, and went to make war with the remnant of her seed, which keep the commandments of God, and have the testimony of Jesus Christ." Rev. 12:17.

But "every plant, which My heavenly Father hath not planted, shall be rooted up." In place of the authority of the so-called fathers of the church, God bids us accept the word of the eternal Father, the Lord of heaven and earth. Here alone is truth unmixed with error. David said, "I have more understanding than all my teachers: for Thy testimonies are my meditation. I understand more than the ancients, because I keep Thy precepts." Ps. 119:99, 100. Let all who accept human authority, the customs of the church, or the traditions of the fathers, take heed to the warning conveyed in the words of Christ, "In vain they do worship Me, teaching for doctrines the commandments of men."

5

Barriers Broken Down

This chapter is based on Matthew 15:21-28; Mark 7:24-30.

After the encounter with the Pharisees, Jesus withdrew from Capernaum, and crossing Galilee, repaired to the hill country on the borders of Phoenicia. Looking westward, He could see, spread out upon the plain below, the ancient cities of Tyre and Sidon, with their heathen temples, their magnificent palaces and marts of trade, and the harbors filled with shipping. Beyond was the blue expanse of the Mediterranean, over which the messengers of the gospel were to bear its glad tidings to the centers of the world's great empire. But the time was not yet. The work before Him now was to prepare His disciples for their mission. In coming to this region He hoped to find the retirement He had failed to secure at Bethsaida. Yet this was not His only purpose in taking this journey.

"Behold, a Canaanitish woman came out from those borders, and cried, saying, Have mercy on me, O Lord, Thou Son of David; my daughter is grievously vexed with a devil." Matt. 15:22, R. V. The people of this district were of the old Canaanite race. They were idolaters, and were despised and hated by the Jews. To this class belonged the woman who now came to Jesus. She was a heathen, and was therefore excluded from the advantages which the Jews daily enjoyed. There were many Jews living among the Phoenicians, and the tidings of Christ's work had penetrated to this region. Some of the people had listened to His words and had witnessed His wonderful works. This woman had heard of the prophet, who, it was reported, healed all manner of diseases. As she heard of His power, hope sprang up in her heart. Inspired by a mother's love, she determined to present her daughter's case to Him. It was her resolute purpose to bring her affliction to Jesus. He must heal her child. She had sought help from the heathen gods, but had obtained no relief. And at times she was tempted to think, What can this Jewish teacher do for me? But the word had come, He heals all manner of diseases, whether those who come to Him for help are rich or poor. She determined not to lose her only hope.

Christ knew this woman's situation. He knew that she was longing to see Him, and He placed Himself in her path. By ministering to her sorrow, He could give a living representation of the lesson He designed to teach. For this He had brought His disciples into this region. He desired them to see the ignorance existing in cities and villages close to the land of Israel. The people who had been given every opportunity to understand the truth were without a knowledge of the needs of those around them. No effort was made to help souls in darkness. The partition wall which Jewish pride had erected, shut even the disciples from sympathy with the heathen world. But these barriers were to be broken down.

Christ did not immediately reply to the woman's request. He received this representative of a despised race as the Jews would have done. In this He designed that His disciples should be impressed with the cold and heartless manner in which the Jews would treat such a case, as evinced by His reception of the woman, and the compassionate manner in which He would have them deal with such distress, as manifested by His subsequent granting of her petition.

But although Jesus did not reply, the woman did not lose faith. As He passed on, as if not hearing her, she followed Him, continuing her supplications. Annoyed by her importunities, the disciples asked Jesus to send her away. They saw that their Master treated her with indifference, and they therefore supposed that the prejudice of the Jews against the Canaanites was pleasing to Him. But it was a pitying Saviour to whom the woman made her plea, and in answer to the request of the disciples, Jesus said, "I am not sent but unto the lost sheep of the house of Israel." Although this answer appeared to be in accordance with the prejudice of the Jews, it was an implied rebuke to the disciples, which they afterward understood as reminding them of what He had often told them,—that He came to the world to save all who would accept Him.

The woman urged her case with increased earnestness, bowing at Christ's feet, and crying, "Lord, help me." Jesus, still apparently rejecting her entreaties, according to the unfeeling prejudice of the Jews, answered, "It is not meet to take the children's bread, and to cast it to dogs." This was virtually asserting that it was not just to lavish the blessings brought to the favored people of God upon strangers and aliens from Israel. This answer would have utterly discouraged a less earnest seeker. But the woman saw that her opportunity had come. Beneath the apparent refusal of Jesus, she saw a compassion that He could not hide. "Truth, Lord," she answered, "yet the dogs eat of the crumbs which fall from their masters' table." While the children of the household eat at the father's table, even the dogs are not left unfed. They have a right to the crumbs that fall from the table abundantly supplied. So while there were many blessings given to Israel, was there not also a blessing for her? She was looked upon as a dog, and had she not then a dog's claim to a crumb from His bounty?

Jesus had just departed from His field of labor because the scribes and Pharisees were seeking to take His life. They murmured and complained. They manifested unbelief and bitterness, and refused the salvation so freely offered them. Here Christ meets one of an unfortunate and despised race, that has not been favored with the light of God's word; yet she yields at once to the divine influence of Christ, and has implicit faith in His ability to grant the favor she asks. She begs for the crumbs that fall from the Master's table. If she may have the privilege of a dog, she is willing to be regarded as a dog. She has no national or religious prejudice or pride to influence her course, and she immediately acknowledges Jesus as the Redeemer, and as being able to do all that she asks of Him.

The Saviour is satisfied. He has tested her faith in Him. By His dealings with her, He has shown that she who has been regarded as an outcast from Israel is no longer an alien, but a child in God's household. As a child it is her privilege to share in the Father's gifts. Christ now grants her request, and finishes the lesson to the disciples. Turning to her with a look of pity and love, He says, "O woman, great is thy faith: be it unto thee even as thou wilt." From that hour her daughter became whole. The demon troubled her no more. The woman departed, acknowledging her Saviour, and happy in the granting of her prayer.

This was the only miracle that Jesus wrought while on this journey. It was for the performance of this act that He went to the borders of Tyre and Sidon. He wished to relieve the afflicted woman, and at the same time to leave an example in His work of mercy toward one of a despised people for the benefit of His disciples when He should no longer be with them. He wished to lead them from their Jewish exclusiveness to be interested in working for others besides their own people.

Jesus longed to unfold the deep mysteries of the truth which had been hid for ages, that the Gentiles should be fellow heirs with the Jews, and "partakers of His promise in Christ by the gospel." Eph. 3:6. This truth the disciples were slow to learn, and the divine Teacher gave them lesson upon lesson. In rewarding the faith of the centurion at Capernaum, and preaching the gospel to the inhabitants of Sychar, He had already given evidence that He did not share the intolerance of the Jews. But the Samaritans had some knowledge of God; and the centurion had shown kindness to Israel. Now Jesus brought the disciples in contact with a heathen, whom they regarded as having no reason above any of her people, to expect favor from Him. He would give an example of how such a one should be treated. The disciples had thought that He dispensed too freely the gifts of His grace. He would show that His love was not to be circumscribed to race or nation.

When He said, "I am not sent but unto the lost sheep of the house of Israel," He stated the truth, and in His work for the Canaanite woman He was fulfilling His commission. This woman was one of the lost sheep that Israel should have rescued. It was their appointed work, the work which they had neglected, that Christ was doing.

This act opened the minds of the disciples more fully to the labor that lay before them among the Gentiles. They saw a wide field of usefulness outside of Judea. They saw souls bearing sorrows unknown to those more highly favored. Among those whom they had been taught to despise were souls longing for help from the mighty Healer, hungering for the light of truth, which had been so abundantly given to the Jews.

Afterward, when the Jews turned still more persistently from the disciples, because they declared Jesus to be the Saviour of the world, and when the partition wall between Jew and Gentile was broken down by the death of Christ, this lesson, and similar ones which pointed to the gospel work unrestricted by custom or nationality, had a powerful influence upon the representatives of Christ, in directing their labors.

The Saviour's visit to Phoenicia and the miracle there performed had a yet wider purpose. Not alone for the afflicted woman, nor even for His disciples and those who received their labors, was the work accomplished; but also "that ye might believe that Jesus is the Christ, the Son of God; and that believing ye might have life through His name." John 20:31. The same agencies that barred men away from Christ eighteen hundred years ago are at work today. The spirit which built up the partition wall between Jew and Gentile is still active. Pride and prejudice have built strong walls of separation between different classes of men. Christ and His mission have been misrepresented, and multitudes feel that they are virtually shut away from the ministry of the gospel. But let them not feel that they are shut away from Christ. There are no barriers which man or Satan can erect but that faith can penetrate.

In faith the woman of Phoenicia flung herself against the barriers that had been piled up between Jew and Gentile. Against discouragement, regardless of appearances that might have led her to doubt, she trusted the Saviour's love. It is thus that Christ desires us to trust in Him. The blessings of salvation are for every soul. Nothing but his own choice can prevent any man from becoming a partaker of the promise in Christ by the gospel.

Caste is hateful to God. He ignores everything of this character. In His sight the souls of all men are of equal value. He "hath made of one blood all nations of men for to dwell on all the face of the earth, and hath determined the times before appointed, and the bounds of their habitation; that they should seek the Lord, if haply they might feel after Him, and find Him, though He be not far from every one of us." Without distinction of age, or rank, or nationality, or religious privilege, all are invited to come unto Him and live. "Whosoever believeth on Him shall not be ashamed. For there is no difference." "There is neither Jew nor Greek, there is neither bond nor free." "The rich and poor meet together: the Lord is the Maker of them all." "The same Lord over all is rich unto all that call upon Him. For whosoever shall call upon the name of the Lord shall be saved." Acts 17:26, 27; Gal. 3:28; Prov. 22:2; Rom. 10:11-13.

6

The True Sign

This chapter is based on Matthew 15:29-39; 16:1-12; Mark 7:31-37; 8:1-21.

Again He went out from the borders of Tyre, and came through Sidon unto the Sea of Galilee, through the midst of the borders of Decapolis." Mark 7:31, R. V.

It was in the region of Decapolis that the demoniacs of Gergesa had been healed. Here the people, alarmed at the destruction of the swine, had constrained Jesus to depart from among them. But they had listened to the messengers He left behind, and a desire was aroused to see Him. As He came again into that region, a crowd gathered about Him, and a deaf, stammering man was brought to Him. Jesus did not, according to His custom, restore the man by a word only. Taking him apart from the multitude, He put His fingers in his ears, and touched his tongue; looking up to heaven, He sighed at thought of the ears that would not be open to the truth, the tongues that refused to acknowledge the Redeemer. At the word, "Be opened," the man's speech was restored, and, disregarding the command to tell no man, he published abroad the story of his cure.

Jesus went up into a mountain, and there the multitude flocked to Him, bringing their sick and lame, and laying them at His feet. He healed them all; and the people, heathen as they were, glorified the God of Israel. For three days they continued to throng about the Saviour, sleeping at night in the open air, and through the day pressing eagerly to hear the words of Christ, and to see His works. At the end of three days their food was spent. Jesus would not send them away hungry, and He called upon His disciples to give them food. Again the disciples revealed their unbelief. At Bethsaida they had seen how, with Christ's blessing, their little store availed for the feeding of the multitude; yet they did not now bring forward their all, trusting His power to multiply it for the hungry crowds. Moreover, those whom He fed at Bethsaida were Jews; these were Gentiles and heathen. Jewish prejudice was still strong in the hearts of the disciples, and they answered Jesus, "Whence can a man satisfy these men with bread here in the wilderness?" But obedient to His word they brought Him what they had,—seven loaves and two fishes. The multitude were fed, seven large baskets of fragments remaining. Four thousand men, besides women and children, were thus refreshed, and Jesus sent them away with glad and grateful hearts.

Then taking a boat with His disciples, He crossed the lake to Magdala, at the southern end of the plain of Gennesaret. In the border of Tyre and Sidon His spirit had been refreshed by the confiding trust of the Syrophoenician woman. The heathen people of Decapolis had received Him with gladness. Now as He landed once more in Galilee, where His power had been most strikingly manifested, where most of His works of mercy had been performed, and His teaching given, He was met with contemptuous unbelief.

A deputation of Pharisees had been joined by representatives from the rich and lordly Sadducees, the party of the priests, the skeptics and aristocracy of the nation. The two sects had been at bitter enmity. The Sadducees courted the favor of the ruling power in order to maintain their own position and authority. The Pharisees, on the other hand, fostered the popular hatred against the Romans, longing for the time when they could throw off the yoke of the conqueror. But Pharisee and Sadducee now united against Christ. Like seeks like; and evil, wherever it exists, leagues with evil for the destruction of the good.

Now the Pharisees and Sadducees came to Christ, asking for a sign from heaven. When in the days of Joshua Israel went out to battle with the Canaanites at Bethhoron, the sun had stood still at the leader's command until victory was gained; and many similar wonders had been manifest in their history. Some such sign was demanded of Jesus. But these signs were not what the Jews needed.

No mere external evidence could benefit them. What they needed was not intellectual enlightenment, but spiritual renovation.

"O ye hypocrites," said Jesus, "ye can discern the face of the sky,"—by studying the sky they could foretell the weather,—"but can ye not discern the signs of the times?" Christ's own words, spoken with the power of the Holy Spirit that convicted them of sin, were the sign that God had given for their salvation. And signs direct from heaven had been given to attest the mission of Christ. The song of the angels to the shepherds, the star that guided the wise men, the dove and the voice from heaven at His baptism, were witnesses for Him.

"And He sighed deeply in His spirit, and saith, Why doth this generation seek after a sign?" "There shall no sign be given unto it, but the sign of the prophet Jonas." As Jonah was three days and three nights in the belly of the whale, Christ was to be the same time "in the heart of the earth." And as the preaching of Jonah was a sign to the Ninevites, so Christ's preaching was a sign to His generation. But what a contrast in the reception of the word! The people of the great heathen city trembled as they heard the warning from God. Kings and nobles humbled themselves; the high and the lowly together cried to the God of heaven, and His mercy was granted unto them. "The men of Nineveh shall rise in judgment with this generation," Christ had said, "and shall condemn it: because they repented at the preaching of Jonas; and, behold, a greater than Jonas is here." Matt. 12:40, 41.

Every miracle that Christ performed was a sign of His divinity. He was doing the very work that had been foretold of the Messiah; but to the Pharisees these works of mercy were a positive offense. The Jewish leaders looked with heartless indifference on human suffering. In many cases their selfishness and oppression had caused the affliction that Christ relieved. Thus His miracles were to them a reproach.

That which led the Jews to reject the Saviour's work was the highest evidence of His divine character. The greatest significance of His miracles is seen in the fact that they were for the blessing of humanity. The highest evidence that He came from God is that His life revealed the character of God. He did the works and spoke the words of God. Such a life is the greatest of all miracles.

When the message of truth is presented in our day, there are many who, like the Jews, cry, Show us a sign. Work us a miracle. Christ wrought no miracle at the demand of the Pharisees. He wrought no miracle in the wilderness in answer to Satan's insinuations. He does not impart to us power to vindicate ourselves or to satisfy the demands of unbelief and pride. But the gospel is not without a sign of its divine origin. Is it not a miracle that we can break from the bondage of Satan? Enmity against Satan is not natural to the human heart; it is implanted by the grace of God. When one who has been controlled by a stubborn, wayward will is set free, and yields himself wholeheartedly to the drawing of God's heavenly agencies, a miracle is wrought; so also when a man who has been under strong delusion comes to understand moral truth. Every time a soul is converted, and learns to love God and keep His commandments, the promise of God is fulfilled, "A new heart also will I give you, and a new spirit will I put within you." Ezek. 36:26. The change in human hearts, the transformation of human characters, is a miracle that reveals an ever-living Saviour, working to rescue souls. A consistent life in Christ is a great miracle. In the preaching of the word of God, the sign that should be manifest now and always is the presence of the Holy Spirit, to make the word a regenerating power to those that hear. This is God's witness before the world to the divine mission of His Son.

Those who desired a sign from Jesus had so hardened their hearts in unbelief that they did not discern in His character the likeness of God. They would not see that His mission was in fulfillment of the Scriptures. In the parable of the rich man and Lazarus, Jesus said to the Pharisees, "If they hear not Moses and the prophets, neither will they be persuaded, though one rose from the dead." Luke 16:31. No sign that could be given in heaven or earth would benefit them.

Jesus "sighed deeply in His spirit," and, turning from the group of cavilers, re-entered the boat with His disciples. In sorrowful silence they again crossed the lake. They did not, however, return to the place they had left, but directed their course toward Bethsaida, near where the five thousand had been fed. Upon reaching the farther side, Jesus said, "Take heed and beware of the leaven of the

Pharisees and of the Sadducees." The Jews had been accustomed since the days of Moses to put away leaven from their houses at the Passover season, and they had thus been taught to regard it as a type of sin. Yet the disciples failed to understand Jesus. In their sudden departure from Magdala they had forgotten to take bread, and they had with them only one loaf. To this circumstance they understood Christ to refer, warning them not to buy bread of a Pharisee or a Sadducee. Their lack of faith and spiritual insight had often led them to similar misconception of His words. Now Jesus reproved them for thinking that He who had fed thousands with a few fishes and barley loaves could in that solemn warning have referred merely to temporal food. There was danger that the crafty reasoning of the Pharisees and the Sadducees would leaven His disciples with unbelief, causing them to think lightly of the works of Christ.

The disciples were inclined to think that their Master should have granted the demand for a sign in the heavens. They believed that He was fully able to do this, and that such a sign would put His enemies to silence. They did not discern the hypocrisy of these cavilers.

Months afterward, "when there were gathered together an innumerable multitude of people, insomuch that they trode one upon another," Jesus repeated the same teaching. "He began to say unto His disciples first of all, Beware ye of the leaven of the Pharisees, which is hypocrisy." Luke 12:1.

The leaven placed in the meal works imperceptibly, changing the whole mass to its own nature. So if hypocrisy is allowed to exist in the heart, it permeates the character and the life. A striking example of the hypocrisy of the Pharisees, Christ had already rebuked in denouncing the practice of "Corban," by which a neglect of filial duty was concealed under a pretense of liberality to the temple. The scribes and Pharisees were insinuating deceptive principles. They concealed the real tendency of their doctrines, and improved every occasion to instill them artfully into the minds of their hearers. These false principles, when once accepted, worked like leaven in the meal, permeating and transforming the character. It was this deceptive teaching that made it so hard for the people to receive the words of Christ.

The same influences are working today through those who try to explain the law of God in such a way as to make it conform to their practices. This class do not attack the law openly, but put forward speculative theories that undermine its principles. They explain it so as to destroy its force.

The hypocrisy of the Pharisees was the product of self-seeking. The glorification of themselves was the object of their lives. It was this that led them to pervert and misapply the Scriptures, and blinded them to the purpose of Christ's mission. This subtle evil even the disciples of Christ were in danger of cherishing. Those who classed themselves with the followers of Jesus, but who had not left all in order to become His disciples, were influenced in a great degree by the reasoning of the Pharisees. They were often vacillating between faith and unbelief, and they did not discern the treasures of wisdom hidden in Christ. Even the disciples, though outwardly they had left all for Jesus' sake, had not in heart ceased to seek great things for themselves. It was this spirit that prompted the strife as to who should be greatest. It was this that came between them and Christ, making them so little in sympathy with His mission of self-sacrifice, so slow to comprehend the mystery of redemption. As leaven, if left to complete its work, will cause corruption and decay, so does the self-seeking spirit, cherished, work the defilement and ruin of the soul.

Among the followers of our Lord today, as of old, how widespread is this subtle, deceptive sin! How often our service to Christ, our communion with one another, is marred by the secret desire to exalt self! How ready the thought of self-gratulation, and the longing for human approval! It is the love of self, the desire for an easier way than God has appointed that leads to the substitution of human theories and traditions for the divine precepts. To His own disciples the warning words of Christ are spoken, "Take heed and beware of the leaven of the Pharisees."

The religion of Christ is sincerity itself. Zeal for God's glory is the motive implanted by the Holy Spirit; and only the effectual working of the Spirit can implant this motive. Only the power of God can banish self-seeking and hypocrisy. This change is the sign of His working. When the faith we accept destroys selfishness and pretense, when it leads us to seek God's glory and not our own, we may know that it is of the right order. "Father, glorify Thy name" (John 12:28), was the keynote of Christ's life, and if we follow Him, this will be the keynote of our life. He commands us to "walk, even as He walked;" and "hereby we do know that we know Him, if we keep His commandments."1 John 2:6, 3.

7

He Was Transfigured

This chapter is based on Matthew 17:1-8; Mark 9:2-8; Luke 9:28-36.

Evening is drawing on as Jesus calls to His side three of His disciples, Peter, James, and John, and leads them across the fields, and far up a rugged path, to a lonely mountainside. The Saviour and His disciples have spent the day in traveling and teaching, and the mountain climb adds to their weariness. Christ has lifted burdens from mind and body of many sufferers; He has sent the thrill of life through their enfeebled frames; but He also is compassed with humanity, and with His disciples He is wearied with the ascent.

The light of the setting sun still lingers on the mountain top, and gilds with its fading glory the path they are traveling. But soon the light dies out from hill as well as valley, the sun disappears behind the western horizon, and the solitary travelers are wrapped in the darkness of night. The gloom of their surroundings seems in harmony with their sorrowful lives, around which the clouds are gathering and thickening.

The disciples do not venture to ask Christ whither He is going, or for what purpose. He has often spent entire nights in the mountains in prayer. He whose hand formed mountain and valley is at home with nature, and enjoys its quietude. The disciples follow where Christ leads the way; yet they wonder why their Master should lead them up this toilsome ascent when they are weary, and when He too is in need of rest.

Presently Christ tells them that they are now to go no farther.

Stepping a little aside from them, the Man of Sorrows pours out His supplications with strong crying and tears. He prays for strength to endure the test in behalf of humanity. He must Himself gain a fresh hold on Omnipotence, for only thus can He contemplate the future. And He pours out His heart longings for His disciples, that in the hour of the power of darkness their faith may not fail. The dew is heavy upon His bowed form, but He heeds it not. The shadows of night gather thickly about Him, but He regards not their gloom. So the hours pass slowly by. At first the disciples unite their prayers with His in sincere devotion; but after a time they are overcome with weariness, and, even while trying to retain their interest in the scene, they fall asleep. Jesus has told them of His sufferings; He has taken them with Him that they might unite with Him in prayer; even now He is praying for them. The Saviour has seen the gloom of His disciples, and has longed to lighten their grief by an assurance that their faith has not been in vain. Not all, even of the twelve, can receive the revelation He desires to give. Only the three who are to witness His anguish in Gethsemane have been chosen to be with Him on the mount. Now the burden of His prayer is that they may be given a manifestation of the glory He had with the Father before the world was, that His kingdom may be revealed to human eyes, and that His disciples may be strengthened to behold it. He pleads that they may witness a manifestation of His divinity that will comfort them in the hour of His supreme agony with the knowledge that He is of a surety the Son of God and that His shameful death is a part of the plan of redemption.

His prayer is heard. While He is bowed in lowliness upon the stony ground, suddenly the heavens open, the golden gates of the city of God are thrown wide, and holy radiance descends upon the mount, enshrouding the Saviour's form. Divinity from within flashes through humanity, and meets the glory coming from above. Arising from His prostrate position, Christ stands in godlike majesty. The soul agony is gone. His countenance now shines "as the sun," and His garments are "white as the light."

The disciples, awaking, behold the flood of glory that illuminates the mount. In fear and amazement they gaze upon the radiant form of their Master. As they become able to endure the wondrous light, they see that Jesus is not alone. Beside Him are two heavenly beings, in close converse with Him. They are Moses, who upon Sinai had talked with God; and Elijah, to whom the high privilege was given—granted to but one other of the sons of Adam—never to come under the power of death.

Upon Mount Pisgah fifteen centuries before, Moses had stood gazing upon the Land of Promise. But because of his sin at Meribah, it was not for him to enter there. Not for him was the joy of leading the host of Israel into the inheritance of their fathers. His agonized entreaty, "I pray Thee, let me go over, and see the good land that is beyond Jordan, that goodly mountain, and Lebanon" (Deut. 3:25), was refused. The hope that for forty years had lighted up the darkness of the desert wanderings must be denied. A wilderness grave was the goal of those years of toil and heart-burdening care. But He who is "able to do exceeding abundantly above all that we ask or think" (Eph. 3:20), had in this measure answered His servant's prayer. Moses passed under the dominion of death, but he was not to remain in the tomb. Christ Himself called him forth to life. Satan the tempter had claimed the body of Moses because of his sin; but Christ the Saviour brought him forth from the grave. Jude 9.

Moses upon the mount of transfiguration was a witness to Christ's victory over sin and death. He represented those who shall come forth from the grave at the resurrection of the just. Elijah, who had been translated to heaven without seeing death, represented those who will be living upon the earth at Christ's second coming, and who will be "changed, in a moment, in the twinkling of an eye, at the last trump;" when "this mortal must put on immortality," and "this corruptible must put on incorruption." 1 Cor. 15:51-53. Jesus was clothed with the light of heaven, as He will appear when He shall come "the second time without sin unto salvation." For He will come "in the glory of His Father with the holy angels." Heb. 9:28; Mark 8:38. The Saviour's promise to the disciples was now fulfilled. Upon the mount the future kingdom of glory was represented in miniature,—Christ the King, Moses a representative of the risen saints, and Elijah of the translated ones.

The disciples do not yet comprehend the scene; but they rejoice that the patient Teacher, the meek and lowly One, who has wandered to and fro a helpless stranger, is honored by the favored ones of heaven. They believe that Elijah has come to announce the Messiah's reign, and that the kingdom of Christ is about to be set up on the earth. The memory of their fear and disappointment they would banish forever. Here, where the glory of God is revealed, they long to tarry. Peter exclaims, "Master, it is good for us to be here: and let us make three tabernacles; one for Thee, and one for Moses, and one for Elias." The disciples are confident that Moses and Elijah have been sent to protect their Master, and to establish His authority as king.

But before the crown must come the cross. Not the inauguration of Christ as king, but the decease to be accomplished at Jerusalem, is the subject of their conference with Jesus. Bearing the weakness of humanity, and burdened with its sorrow and sin, Jesus walked alone in the midst of men. As the darkness of the coming trial pressed upon Him, He was in loneliness of spirit, in a world that knew Him not. Even His loved disciples, absorbed in their own doubt and sorrow and ambitious hopes, had not comprehended the mystery of His mission. He had dwelt amid the love and fellowship of heaven; but in the world that He had created, He was in solitude. Now heaven had sent its messengers to Jesus; not angels, but men who had endured suffering and sorrow, and who could sympathize with the Saviour in the trial of His earthly life. Moses and Elijah had been colaborers with Christ. They had shared His longing for the salvation of men. Moses had pleaded for Israel: "Yet now, if Thou wilt forgive their sin—; and if not, blot me, I pray Thee, out of Thy book which Thou hast written." Ex. 32:32. Elijah had known loneliness of spirit, as for three years and a half of famine he had borne the burden of the nation's hatred and its woe. Alone he had stood for God upon Mount Carmel. Alone he had fled to the desert in anguish and despair. These men, chosen above every angel around the throne, had come to commune with Jesus concerning the scenes of His suffering, and to comfort Him with the assurance of the sympathy of heaven. The hope of the world, the salvation of every human being, was the burden of their interview.

Through being overcome with sleep, the disciples heard little of what passed between Christ and the heavenly messengers. Failing to watch and pray, they had not received that which God desired to give them,—a knowledge of the sufferings of Christ, and the glory that should follow. They lost the blessing that might have been theirs through sharing His self-sacrifice. Slow of heart to believe were these disciples, little appreciative of the treasure with which Heaven sought to enrich them.

Yet they received great light. They were assured that all heaven knew of the sin of the Jewish nation in rejecting Christ. They were given a clearer insight into the work of the Redeemer. They saw with their eyes and heard with their ears things that were beyond the comprehension of man. They were "eyewitnesses of His majesty" (2 Peter 1:16), and they realized that Jesus was indeed the Messiah, to whom patriarchs and prophets had witnessed, and that He was recognized as such by the heavenly universe.

While they were still gazing on the scene upon the mount, "a bright cloud overshadowed them: and behold a voice out of the cloud, which said, This is My beloved Son, in whom I am well pleased; hear ye Him." As they beheld the cloud of glory, brighter than that which went before the tribes of Israel in the wilderness; as they heard the voice of God speak in awful majesty that caused the mountain to tremble, the disciples fell smitten to the earth. They remained prostrate, their faces hidden, till Jesus came near, and touched them, dispelling their fears with His well-known voice, "Arise, and be not afraid." Venturing to lift up their eyes, they saw that the heavenly glory had passed away, the forms of Moses and Elijah had disappeared. They were upon the mount, alone with Jesus.

8

Ministry

This chapter is based on Matthew 17:9-21; Mark 9:9-29; Luke 9:37-45.

The entire night had been passed in the mountain; and as the sun arose, Jesus and His disciples descended to the plain. Absorbed in thought, the disciples were awed and silent. Even Peter had not a word to say. Gladly would they have lingered in that holy place which had been touched with the light of heaven, and where the Son of God had manifested His glory; but there was work to be done for the people, who were already searching far and near for Jesus.

At the foot of the mountain a large company had gathered, led hither by the disciples who had remained behind, but who knew whither Jesus had resorted. As the Saviour drew near, He charged His three companions to keep silence concerning what they had witnessed, saying, "Tell the vision to no man, until the Son of man be risen again from the dead." The revelation made to the disciples was to be pondered in their own hearts, not to be published abroad. To relate it to the multitudes would excite only ridicule or idle wonder. And even the nine apostles would not understand the scene until after Christ had risen from the dead. How slow of comprehension even the three favored disciples were, is seen in the fact that notwithstanding all that Christ had said of what was before Him, they queried among themselves what the rising from the dead should mean. Yet they asked no explanation from Jesus. His words in regard to the future had filled them with sorrow; they sought no further revelation concerning that which they were fain to believe might never come to pass.

As the people on the plain caught sight of Jesus, they ran to meet Him, greeting Him with expressions of reverence and joy. Yet His quick eye discerned that they were in great perplexity. The disciples appeared troubled. A circumstance had just occurred that had caused them bitter disappointment and humiliation.

While they were waiting at the foot of the mountain, a father had brought to them his son, to be delivered from a dumb spirit that tormented him. Authority over unclean spirits, to cast them out, had been conferred on the disciples when Jesus sent out the twelve to preach through Galilee. As they went forth strong in faith, the evil spirits had obeyed their word. Now in the name of Christ they commanded the torturing spirit to leave his victim; but the demon only mocked them by a fresh display of his power. The disciples, unable to account for their defeat, felt that they were bringing dishonor upon themselves and their Master. And in the crowd there were scribes who made the most of this opportunity to humiliate them. Pressing around the disciples, they plied them with questions, seeking to prove that they and their Master were deceivers. Here, the rabbis triumphantly declared, was an evil spirit that neither the disciples nor Christ Himself could conquer. The people were inclined to side with the scribes, and a feeling of contempt and scorn pervaded the crowd.

But suddenly the accusations ceased. Jesus and the three disciples were seen approaching, and with a quick revulsion of feeling the people turned to meet them. The night of communion with the heavenly glory had left its trace upon the Saviour and His companions. Upon their countenances was a light that awed the beholders. The scribes drew back in fear, while the people welcomed Jesus.

As if He had been a witness of all that had occurred, the Saviour came to the scene of conflict, and fixing His gaze upon the scribes inquired, "What question ye with them?"

But the voices so bold and defiant before were now silent. A hush had fallen upon the entire company. Now the afflicted father made his way through the crowd, and falling at the feet of Jesus, poured out the story of his trouble and disappointment.

"Master," he said, "I have brought unto Thee my son, which hath a dumb spirit; and wheresoever he taketh him, he teareth him: . . . and I spake to Thy disciples that they should cast him out; and they could not."

Jesus looked about Him upon the awe-stricken multitude, the caviling scribes, the perplexed disciples. He read the unbelief in every heart; and in a voice filled with sorrow He exclaimed, "O faithless generation, how long shall I be with you? how long shall I suffer you?" Then He bade the distressed father, "Bring thy son hither."

The boy was brought, and as the Saviour's eyes fell upon him, the evil spirit cast him to the ground in convulsions of agony. He lay wallowing and foaming, rending the air with unearthly shrieks.

Again the Prince of life and the prince of the powers of darkness had met on the field of battle,—Christ in fulfillment of His mission to "preach deliverance to the captives, . . . to set at liberty them that are bruised" (Luke 4:18), Satan seeking to hold his victim under his control. Angels of light and the hosts of evil angels, unseen, were pressing near to behold the conflict. For a moment, Jesus permitted the evil spirit to display his power, that the beholders might comprehend the deliverance about to be wrought.

The multitude looked on with bated breath, the father in an agony of hope and fear. Jesus asked, "How long is it ago since this came unto him?" The father told the story of long years of suffering, and then, as if he could endure no more, exclaimed, "If Thou canst do anything, have compassion on us, and help us." "If Thou canst!" Even now the father questioned the power of Christ.

Jesus answers, "If thou canst believe, all things are possible to him that believeth." There is no lack of power on the part of Christ; the healing of the son depends upon the father's faith. With a burst of tears, realizing his own weakness, the father casts himself upon Christ's mercy, with the cry, "Lord, I believe; help Thou mine unbelief."

Jesus turns to the suffering one, and says, "Thou dumb and deaf spirit, I charge thee, come out of him, and enter no more into him." There is a cry, an agonized struggle. The demon, in passing, seems about to rend the life from his victim. Then the boy lies motionless, and apparently lifeless. The multitude whisper, "He is dead." But Jesus takes him by the hand, and lifting him up, presents him, in perfect soundness of mind and body, to his father. Father and son praise the name of their Deliverer. The multitude are "amazed at the mighty power of God," while the scribes, defeated and crestfallen, turn sullenly away.

"If Thou canst do anything, have compassion on us, and help us." How many a sin-burdened soul has echoed that prayer. And to all, the pitying Saviour's answer is, "If thou canst believe, all things are possible to him that believeth." It is faith that connects us with heaven, and brings us strength for coping with the powers of darkness. In Christ, God has provided means for subduing every sinful trait, and resisting every temptation, however strong. But many feel that they lack faith, and therefore they remain away from Christ. Let these souls, in their helpless unworthiness, cast themselves upon the mercy of their compassionate Saviour. Look not to self, but to Christ. He who healed the sick and cast out demons when He walked among men is the same mighty Redeemer today. Faith comes by the word of God. Then grasp His promise, "Him that cometh to Me I will in no wise cast out." John 6:37. Cast yourself at His feet with the cry, "Lord, I believe; help *Thou* mine unbelief." You can never perish while you do this—never.

In a brief space of time the favored disciples have beheld the extreme of glory and of humiliation. They have seen humanity as transfigured into the image of God, and as debased into the likeness of Satan. From the mountain where He has talked with the heavenly messengers, and has been proclaimed the Son of God by the voice from the radiant glory, they have seen Jesus descend to meet that most distressing and revolting spectacle, the maniac boy, with distorted countenance, gnashing his teeth in spasms of agony that no human power could relieve. And this mighty Redeemer, who but a few hours before stood glorified before His wondering disciples, stoops to lift the victim of Satan from the earth where he is wallowing, and in health of mind and body restores him to his father and his home.

It was an object lesson of redemption,—the Divine One from the Father's glory stooping to save the lost. It represented also the disciples' mission. Not alone upon the mountaintop with Jesus, in hours of spiritual illumination, is the life of Christ's servants to be spent. There is work for them down in the plain. Souls whom Satan has enslaved are waiting for the word of faith and prayer to set them free.

The nine disciples were yet pondering upon the bitter fact of their own failure; and when Jesus was once more alone with them, they questioned, "Why could not we cast him out?" Jesus answered them, "Because of your unbelief: for verily I say unto you, If ye have faith as a grain of mustard seed, ye shall say unto this mountain, Remove hence to yonder place; and it shall remove; and nothing shall be impossible unto you. Howbeit this kind goeth not out but by prayer and fasting." Their unbelief, that shut them out from deeper sympathy with Christ, and the carelessness with which they regarded the sacred work committed to them, had caused their failure in the conflict with the powers of darkness.

The words of Christ pointing to His death had brought sadness and doubt. And the selection of the three disciples to accompany Jesus to the mountain had excited the jealousy of the nine. Instead of strengthening their faith by prayer and meditation on the words of Christ, they had been dwelling on their discouragements and personal grievances. In this state of darkness they had undertaken the conflict with Satan.

In order to succeed in such a conflict they must come to the work in a different spirit. Their faith must be strengthened by fervent prayer and fasting, and humiliation of heart. They must be emptied of self, and be filled with the Spirit and power of God. Earnest, persevering supplication to God in faith—faith that leads to entire dependence upon God, and unreserved consecration to His work—can alone avail to bring men the Holy Spirit's aid in the battle against principalities and powers, the rulers of the darkness of this world, and wicked spirits in high places.

"If ye have faith as a grain of mustard seed," said Jesus, "ye shall say unto this mountain, Remove hence to yonder place; and it shall remove." Though the grain of mustard seed is so small, it contains that same mysterious life principle which produces growth in the loftiest tree. When the mustard seed is cast into the ground, the tiny germ lays hold of every element that God has provided for its nutriment, and it speedily develops a sturdy growth. If you have faith like this, you will lay hold upon God's word, and upon all the helpful agencies He has appointed. Thus your faith will strengthen, and will bring to your aid the power of heaven. The obstacles that are piled by Satan across your path, though apparently as insurmountable as the eternal hills, shall disappear before the demand of faith. "Nothing shall be impossible unto you."

9

Who Is the Greatest?

This chapter is based on Matthew 17:22-27; 18:1-20; Mark 9:30-50; Luke 9:46-48.

On returning to Capernaum, Jesus did not repair to the well-known resorts where He had taught the people, but with His disciples quietly sought the house that was to be His temporary home. During the remainder of His stay in Galilee it was His object to instruct the disciples rather than to labor for the multitudes.

On the journey through Galilee, Christ had again tried to prepare the minds of His disciples for the scenes before Him. He told them that He was to go up to Jerusalem to be put to death and to rise again. And He added the strange and solemn announcement that He was to be betrayed into the hands of His enemies. The disciples did not even now comprehend His words. Although the shadow of a great sorrow fell upon them, a spirit of rivalry found a place in their hearts. They disputed among themselves which should be accounted greatest in the kingdom. This strife they thought to conceal from Jesus, and they did not, as usual, press close to His side, but loitered behind, so that He was in advance of them as they entered Capernaum. Jesus read their thoughts, and He longed to counsel and instruct them. But for this He awaited a quiet hour, when their hearts should be open to receive His words.

Soon after they reached the town, the collector of the temple revenue came to Peter with the question, "Doth not your Master pay tribute?" This tribute was not a civil tax, but a religious contribution, which every Jew was required to pay annually for the support of the temple. A refusal to pay the tribute would be regarded as disloyalty to the temple,—in the estimation of the rabbis a most grievous sin. The Saviour's attitude toward the rabbinical laws, and His plain reproofs to the defenders of tradition, afforded a pretext for the charge that He was seeking to overthrow the temple service. Now His enemies saw an opportunity of casting discredit upon Him. In the collector of the tribute they found a ready ally.

Peter saw in the collector's question an insinuation touching Christ's loyalty to the temple. Zealous for his Master's honor, he hastily answered, without consulting Him, that Jesus would pay the tribute.

But Peter only partially comprehended the purpose of his questioner. There were some classes who were held to be exempt from the payment of the tribute. In the time of Moses, when the Levites were set apart for the service of the sanctuary, they were given no inheritance among the people. The Lord said, "Levi hath no part nor inheritance with his brethren; the Lord is his inheritance." Deut. 10:9. In the days of Christ the priests and Levites were still regarded as especially devoted to the temple, and were not required to make the annual contribution for its support. Prophets also were exempted from this payment. In requiring the tribute from Jesus, the rabbis were setting aside His claim as a prophet or teacher, and were dealing with Him as with any commonplace person. A refusal on His part to pay the tribute would be represented as disloyalty to the temple; while, on the other hand, the payment of it would be taken as justifying their rejection of Him as a prophet.

Only a little before, Peter had acknowledged Jesus as the Son of God; but he now missed an opportunity of setting forth the character of his Master. By his answer to the collector, that Jesus would pay the tribute, he had virtually sanctioned the false conception of Him to which the priests and rulers were trying to give currency.

When Peter entered the house, the Saviour made no reference to what had taken place, but inquired, "What thinkest thou, Simon? of whom do the kings of the earth take custom or tribute? of their own children, or of strangers?" Peter answered, "Of strangers." And Jesus said, "Then are the children free." While the people of a country are taxed for the maintenance of their king, the monarch's own children are exempt. So Israel, the professed people of God, were required to maintain His service; but Jesus, the Son of God, was under no such obligation. If priests and Levites were exempt because of their connection with the temple, how much more He to whom the temple was His Father's house.

If Jesus had paid the tribute without a protest, He would virtually have acknowledged the justice of the claim, and would thus have denied His divinity. But while He saw good to meet the demand, He denied the claim upon which it was based. In providing for the payment of the tribute He gave evidence of His divine character. It was made manifest that He was one with God, and therefore was not under tribute as a mere subject of the kingdom.

"Go thou to the sea," He directed Peter, "and cast an hook, and take up the fish that first cometh up; and when thou hast opened his mouth, thou shalt find a piece of money: that take, and give unto them for Me and thee."

Though He had clothed His divinity with humanity, in this miracle He revealed His glory. It was evident that this was He who through David had declared, "Every beast of the forest is Mine, and the cattle upon a thousand hills. I know all the fowls of the mountains; and the wild beasts of the field are Mine. If I were hungry, I would not tell thee: for the world is Mine, and the fullness thereof." Ps. 50:10-12.

While Jesus made it plain that He was under no obligation to pay the tribute, He entered into no controversy with the Jews in regard to the matter; for they would have misinterpreted His words, and turned them against Him. Lest He should give offense by withholding the tribute, He did that which He could not justly be required to do. This lesson would be of great value to His disciples. Marked changes were soon to take place in their relation to the temple service, and Christ taught them not to place themselves needlessly in antagonism to established order. So far as possible, they were to avoid giving occasion for misinterpretation of their faith. While Christians are not to sacrifice one principle of truth, they should avoid controversy whenever it is possible to do so.

When Christ and the disciples were alone in the house, while Peter was gone to the sea, Jesus called the others to Him, and asked,

"What was it that ye disputed among yourselves by the way?" The presence of Jesus, and His question, put the matter in an entirely different light from that in which it had appeared to them while they were contending by the way. Shame and self-condemnation kept them silent. Jesus had told them that He was to die for their sake, and their selfish ambition was in painful contrast to His unselfish love.

When Jesus told them that He was to be put to death and to rise again, He was trying to draw them into conversation in regard to the great test of their faith. Had they been ready to receive what He desired to make known to them, they would have been saved bitter anguish and despair. His words would have brought consolation in the hour of bereavement and disappointment. But although He had spoken so plainly of what awaited Him, His mention of the fact that He was soon to go to Jerusalem again kindled their hope that the kingdom was about to be set up. This had led to questioning as to who should fill the highest offices. On Peter's return from the sea, the disciples told him of the Saviour's question, and at last one ventured to ask Jesus, "Who is the greatest in the kingdom of heaven?"

The Saviour gathered His disciples about Him, and said to them, "If any man desire to be first, the same shall be last of all, and servant of all." There was in these words a solemnity and impressiveness which the disciples were far from comprehending. That which Christ discerned they could not see. They did not understand the nature of Christ's kingdom, and this ignorance was the apparent cause of their contention. But the real cause lay deeper. By explaining the nature of the kingdom, Christ might for the time have quelled their strife; but this would not have touched the underlying cause. Even after they had received the fullest knowledge, any question of precedence might have renewed the trouble. Thus disaster would have been brought to the church after Christ's departure. The strife for the highest place was the outworking of that same spirit which was the beginning of the great controversy in the worlds above, and which had brought Christ from heaven to die. There rose up before Him a vision of Lucifer, the "son of the morning," in glory surpassing all the angels that surround the throne, and united in closest ties to the Son of God. Lucifer had said, "I will be like the Most High" (Isa. 14:12, 14); and the desire for self-exaltation had brought strife into the heavenly courts, and had banished a multitude of the hosts of God. Had Lucifer really desired to be like the Most High, he would never have deserted his appointed place in heaven; for the spirit of the Most High is manifested in unselfish ministry. Lucifer desired God's power, but not His character. He sought for himself the highest place, and every being who is actuated by his spirit will do the same. Thus alienation, discord, and strife will be inevitable. Dominion becomes the prize of the strongest. The kingdom of Satan is a kingdom of force; every individual regards every other as an obstacle in the way of his own advancement, or a steppingstone on which he himself may climb to a higher place.

While Lucifer counted it a thing to be grasped to be equal with God, Christ, the Exalted One, "made Himself of no reputation, and took upon Him the form of a servant, and was made in the likeness of men: and being found in fashion as a man, He humbled Himself, and became obedient unto death, even the death of the cross." Phil. 2:7, 8. Now the cross was just before Him; and His own disciples were so filled with self-seeking—the very principle of Satan's kingdom—that they could not enter into sympathy with their Lord, or even understand Him as He spoke of His humiliation for them.

Very tenderly, yet with solemn emphasis, Jesus tried to correct the evil. He showed what is the principle that bears sway in the kingdom of heaven, and in what true greatness consists, as estimated by the standard of the courts above. Those who were actuated by pride and love of distinction were thinking of themselves, and of the rewards they were to have, rather than how they were to render back to God the gifts they had received. They would have no place in the kingdom of heaven, for they were identified with the ranks of Satan.

Before honor is humility. To fill a high place before men, Heaven chooses the worker who, like John the Baptist, takes a lowly place before God. The most childlike disciple is the most efficient in labor for God. The heavenly intelligences can co-operate with him who is seeking, not to exalt self, but to save souls. He who feels most deeply his need of divine aid will plead for it; and the Holy Spirit will give unto him glimpses of Jesus that will strengthen and uplift the soul. From communion with Christ he will go forth to work for those who are perishing in their sins. He is anointed for his mission; and he succeeds where many of the learned and intellectually wise would fail.

But when men exalt themselves, feeling that they are a necessity for the success of God's great plan, the Lord causes them to be set aside. It is made evident that the Lord is not dependent upon them. The work does not stop because of their removal from it, but goes forward with greater power.

It was not enough for the disciples of Jesus to be instructed as to the nature of His kingdom. What they needed was a change of heart that would bring them into harmony with its principles. Calling a little child to Him, Jesus set him in the midst of them; then tenderly folding the little one in His arms He said, "Except ye be converted, and become as little children, ye shall not enter into the kingdom of heaven." The simplicity, the self-forgetfulness, and the confiding love of a little child are the attributes that Heaven values. These are the characteristics of real greatness.

Again Jesus explained to the disciples that His kingdom is not characterized by earthly dignity and display. At the feet of Jesus all these distinctions are forgotten. The rich and the poor, the learned and the ignorant, meet together, with no thought of caste or worldly preeminence. All meet as blood-bought souls, alike dependent upon One who has redeemed them to God.

The sincere, contrite soul is precious in the sight of God. He places His own signet upon men, not by their rank, not by their wealth, not by their intellectual greatness, but by their oneness with Christ. The Lord of glory is satisfied with those who are meek and lowly in heart. "Thou hast also given me," said David, "the shield of Thy salvation: . . . and Thy gentleness"—as an element in the human character—"hath made me great." Ps. 18:35.

"Whosoever shall receive one of such children in My name," said Jesus, "receiveth Me: and whosoever shall receive Me, receiveth not Me, but Him that sent Me." "Thus saith the Lord, The heaven is My throne, and the earth is My footstool: . . . but to this man will I look, even to him that is poor and of a contrite spirit, and trembleth at My word." Isa. 66:1, 2.

The Saviour's words awakened in the disciples a feeling of self-distrust. No one had been specially pointed out in the reply; but John was led to question whether in one case his action had been right. With the spirit of a child he laid the matter before Jesus. "Master," he said, "we saw one casting out devils in Thy name, and he followeth not us: and we forbade him, because he followeth not us."

James and John had thought that in checking this man they had had in view their Lord's honor; they began to see that they were jealous for their own. They acknowledged their error, and accepted the reproof of Jesus, "Forbid him not: for there is no man which shall do a miracle in My name, that can lightly speak evil of Me." None who showed themselves in any way friendly to Christ were to be repulsed. There were many who had been deeply moved by the character and the work of Christ, and whose hearts were opening to Him in faith; and the disciples, who could not read motives, must be careful not to discourage these souls. When Jesus was no longer personally among them, and the work was left in their hands, they must not indulge a narrow, exclusive spirit, but manifest the same far-reaching sympathy which they had seen in their Master.

The fact that one does not in all things conform to our personal ideas or opinions will not justify us in forbidding him to labor for God. Christ is the Great Teacher; we are not to judge or to command, but in humility each is to sit at the feet of Jesus, and learn of Him. Every soul whom God has made willing is a channel through which Christ will reveal His pardoning love. How careful we should be lest we discourage one of God's light bearers, and thus intercept the rays that He would have shine to the world!

Harshness or coldness shown by a disciple toward one whom Christ was drawing—such an act as that of John in forbidding one to work miracles in Christ's name—might result in turning the feet into the path of the enemy, and causing the loss of a soul. Rather than for one to do this, said Jesus, "it is better for him that a millstone were hanged about his neck, and he were cast into the sea." And He added, "If thy hand cause thee to stumble, cut it off: it is good for thee to enter into life maimed, rather than having thy two hands to go into hell, into the unquenchable fire. And if thy foot cause thee to stumble, cut it off: it is good for thee to enter into life halt, rather than having thy two feet to be cast into hell." Mark 9:43-45, R. V.

Why this earnest language, than which none can be stronger? Because "the Son of man is come to save that which was lost." Shall His disciples show less regard for the souls of their fellow men than the Majesty of heaven has shown? Every soul has cost an infinite price, and how terrible is the sin of turning one soul away from Christ, so that for him the Saviour's love and humiliation and agony shall have been in vain.

"Woe unto the world because of occasions of stumbling! for it must needs be that the occasions come." Matt. 18:7, R. V. The world, inspired by Satan, will surely oppose the followers of Christ, and seek to destroy their faith; but woe to him who has taken Christ's name, and yet is found doing this work. Our Lord is put to shame by those who claim to serve Him, but who misrepresent His character; and multitudes are deceived, and led into false paths.

Any habit or practice that would lead into sin, and bring dishonor upon Christ, would better be put away, whatever the sacrifice. That which dishonors God cannot benefit the soul. The blessing of heaven cannot attend any man in violating the eternal principles of right. And one sin cherished is sufficient to work the degradation of the character, and to mislead others. If the foot or the hand would be cut off, or even the eye would be plucked out, to save the body from death, how much more earnest should we be to put away sin, that brings death to the soul!

In the ritual service, salt was added to every sacrifice. This, like the offering of incense, signified that only the righteousness of Christ could make the service acceptable to God. Referring to this practice, Jesus said, "Every sacrifice shall be salted with salt." "Have salt in yourselves, and have peace one with another." All who would present themselves "a living sacrifice, holy, acceptable unto God" (Rom. 12:1), must receive the saving salt, the righteousness of our Saviour. Then they become "the salt of the earth," restraining evil among men, as salt preserves from corruption. Matt. 5:13. But if the salt has lost its savor; if there is only a profession of godliness, without the love of Christ, there is no power for good. The life can exert no saving influence upon the world. Your energy and efficiency in the upbuilding of My kingdom, Jesus says, depend upon your receiving of My Spirit. You must be partakers of My grace, in order to be a savor of life unto life. Then there will be no rivalry, no self-seeking, no desire for the highest place. You will have that love which seeks not her own, but another's wealth.

Let the repenting sinner fix his eyes upon "the Lamb of God, which taketh away the sin of the world" (John 1:29); and by beholding, he becomes changed. His fear is turned to joy, his doubts to hope. Gratitude springs up. The stony heart is broken. A tide of love sweeps into the soul. Christ is in him a well of water springing up unto everlasting life. When we see Jesus, a Man of Sorrows and acquainted with grief, working to save the lost, slighted, scorned, derided, driven from city to city till His mission was accomplished; when we behold Him in Gethsemane, sweating great drops of blood, and on the cross dying in agony,—when we see this, self will no longer clamor to be recognized. Looking unto Jesus, we shall be ashamed of our coldness, our lethargy, our self-seeking. We shall be willing to be anything or nothing, so that we may do heart service for the Master. We shall rejoice to bear the cross after Jesus, to endure trial, shame, or persecution for His dear sake.

"We then that are strong ought to bear the infirmities of the weak, and not to please ourselves." Rom. 15:1. No soul who believes in Christ, though his faith may be weak, and his steps wavering as those of a little child, is to be lightly esteemed. By all that has given us advantage over another,—be it education and refinement, nobility of character, Christian training, religious experience,—we are in debt to those less favored; and, so far as lies in our power, we are to minister unto them. If we are strong, we are to stay up the hands of the weak. Angels of glory, that do always behold the face of the Father in heaven, joy in ministering to His little ones. Trembling souls, who have many objectionable traits of character, are their special charge. Angels are ever present where they are most needed, with those who have the hardest battle with self to fight, and whose surroundings are the most discouraging. And in this ministry Christ's true followers will co-operate.

If one of these little ones shall be overcome, and commit a wrong against you, then it is your work to seek his restoration. Do not wait for him to make the first effort for reconciliation. "How think ye?" said Jesus; "if a man have an hundred sheep, and one of them be gone astray, doth he not leave the ninety and nine, and goeth into the mountains, and seeketh that which is gone astray? And if so be that he find it, verily I say unto you, he rejoiceth more of that sheep, than of the ninety and nine which went not astray. Even so it is not the will of your Father which is in heaven, that one of these little ones should perish."

In the spirit of meekness, "considering thyself, lest thou also be tempted," (Gal. 6:1), go to the erring one, and "tell him his fault between thee and him alone." Do not put him to shame by exposing his fault to others, nor bring dishonor upon Christ by making public the sin or error of one who bears His name. Often the truth must be plainly spoken to the erring; he must be led to see his error, that he may reform. But you are not to judge or to condemn. Make no attempt at self-justification. Let all your effort be for his recovery. In treating the wounds of the soul, there is need of the most delicate touch, the finest sensibility. Only the love that flows from the Suffering One of Calvary can avail here. With pitying tenderness, let brother deal with brother, knowing that if you succeed, you will "save a soul from death," and "hide a multitude of sins." James 5:20.

But even this effort may be unavailing. Then, said Jesus, "take with thee one or two more." It may be that their united influence will prevail where that of the first was unsuccessful. Not being parties to the trouble, they will be more likely to act impartially, and this fact will give their counsel greater weight with the erring one.

If he will not hear them, then, and not till then, the matter is to be brought before the whole body of believers. Let the members of the church, as the representatives of Christ, unite in prayer and loving entreaty that the offender may be restored. The Holy Spirit will speak through His servants, pleading with the wanderer to return to God. Paul the apostle, speaking by inspiration, says, "As though God did beseech you by us: we pray you in Christ's stead, be ye reconciled to God." 2 Cor. 5:20. He who rejects this united overture has broken the tie that binds him to Christ, and thus has severed himself from the fellowship of the church. Henceforth, said Jesus, "let him be unto thee as an heathen man and a publican." But he is not to be regarded as cut off from the mercy of God. Let him not be despised or neglected by his former brethren, but be treated with tenderness and compassion, as one of the lost sheep that Christ is still seeking to bring to His fold.

Christ's instruction as to the treatment of the erring repeats in more specific form the teaching given to Israel through Moses: "Thou shalt not hate thy brother in thine heart: thou shalt in anywise rebuke thy neighbor, that thou bear not sin for him." Lev. 19:17, margin. That is, if one neglects the duty Christ has enjoined, of trying to restore those who are in error and sin, he becomes a partaker in the sin. For evils that we might have checked, we are just as responsible as if we were guilty of the acts ourselves.

But it is to the wrongdoer himself that we are to present the wrong. We are not to make it a matter of comment and criticism among ourselves; nor even after it is told to the church, are we at liberty to repeat it to others. A knowledge of the faults of Christians will be only a cause of stumbling to the unbelieving world; and by dwelling upon these things, we ourselves can receive only harm; for it is by beholding that we become changed. While we seek to correct the errors of a brother, the Spirit of Christ will lead us to shield him, as far as possible, from the criticism of even his own brethren, and how much more from the censure of the unbelieving world. We ourselves are erring, and need Christ's pity and forgiveness, and just as we wish Him to deal with us, He bids us deal with one another.

"Whatsoever ye shall bind on earth shall be bound in heaven: and whatsoever ye shall loose on earth shall be loosed in heaven." You are acting as the ambassadors of heaven, and the issues of your work are for eternity.

But we are not to bear this great responsibility alone. Wherever His word is obeyed with a sincere heart, there Christ abides. Not only is He present in the assemblies of the church, but wherever disciples, however few, meet in His name, there also He will be. And He says, "If two of you shall agree on earth as touching anything that they shall ask, it shall be done for them of My Father which is in heaven."

Jesus says, "*My* Father which is in heaven," as reminding His disciples that while by His humanity He is linked with them, a sharer in their trials, and sympathizing with them in their sufferings, by His divinity He is connected with the throne of the Infinite. Wonderful assurance! The heavenly intelligences unite with men in sympathy and labor for the saving of that which was lost. And all the power of heaven is brought to combine with human ability in drawing souls to Christ.

10

At the Feast of Tabernacles

This chapter is based on John 7:1-15, 37-39.

T hree times a year the Jews were required to assemble at Jerusalem for religious purposes. Enshrouded in the pillar of cloud, Israel's invisible Leader had given the directions in regard to these gatherings. During the captivity of the Jews, they could not be observed; but when the people were restored to their own land, the observance of these memorials was once more begun. It was God's design that these anniversaries should call Him to the minds of the people. But with few exceptions, the priests and leaders of the nation had lost sight of this purpose. He who had ordained these national assemblies and understood their significance witnessed their perversion.

The Feast of Tabernacles was the closing gathering of the year. It was God's design that at this time the people should reflect on His goodness and mercy. The whole land had been under His guidance, receiving His blessing. Day and night His watchcare had continued. The sun and rain had caused the earth to produce her fruits. From the valleys and plains of Palestine the harvest had been gathered. The olive berries had been picked, and the precious oil stored in bottles. The palm had yielded her store. The purple clusters of the vine had been trodden in the wine press.

The feast continued for seven days, and for its celebration the inhabitants of Palestine, with many from other lands, left their homes, and came to Jerusalem. From far and near the people came, bringing in their hands a token of rejoicing. Old and young, rich and poor, all brought some gift as a tribute of thanksgiving to Him who had crowned the year with His goodness, and made His paths drop fatness. Everything that could please the eye, and give expression to the universal joy, was brought from the woods; the city bore the appearance of a beautiful forest.

This feast was not only the harvest thanksgiving, but the memorial of God's protecting care over Israel in the wilderness. In commemoration of their tent life, the Israelites during the feast dwelt in booths or tabernacles of green boughs. These were erected in the streets, in the courts of the temple, or on the housetops. The hills and valleys surrounding Jerusalem were also dotted with these leafy dwellings, and seemed to be alive with people.

With sacred song and thanksgiving the worshipers celebrated this occasion. A little before the feast was the Day of Atonement, when, after confession of their sins, the people were declared to be at peace with Heaven. Thus the way was prepared for the rejoicing of the feast. "O give thanks unto the Lord; for He is good: for His mercy endureth forever" (Ps. 106:1) rose triumphantly, while all kinds of music, mingled with shouts of hosanna, accompanied the united singing. The temple was the center of the universal joy. Here was the pomp of the sacrificial ceremonies. Here, ranged on either side of the white marble steps of the sacred building, the choir of Levites led the service of song. The multitude of worshipers, waving their branches of palm and myrtle, took up the strain, and echoed the chorus; and again the melody was caught up by voices near and afar off, till the encircling hills were vocal with praise.

At night the temple and its court blazed with artificial light. The music, the waving of palm branches, the glad hosannas, the great concourse of people, over whom the light streamed from the hanging lamps, the array of the priests, and the majesty of the ceremonies, combined to make a scene that deeply impressed the beholders. But the most impressive ceremony of the feast, one that called forth greatest rejoicing, was one commemorating an event in the wilderness sojourn.

At the first dawn of day, the priests sounded a long, shrill blast upon their silver trumpets, and the answering trumpets, and the glad shouts of the people from their booths, echoing over hill and valley, welcomed the festal day. Then the priest dipped from the flowing waters of the Kedron a flagon of water, and, lifting it on high, while the trumpets were sounding, he ascended the broad steps of the temple, keeping time with the music with slow and measured tread, chanting meanwhile, "Our feet shall stand within thy gates, O Jerusalem." Ps. 122:2.

He bore the flagon to the altar, which occupied a central position in the court of the priests. Here were two silver basins, with a priest standing at each one. The flagon of water was poured into one, and a flagon of wine into the other; and the contents of both flowed into a pipe which communicated with the Kedron, and was conducted to the Dead Sea. This display of the consecrated water represented the fountain that at the command of God had gushed from the rock to quench the thirst of the children of Israel. Then the jubilant strains rang forth, "The Lord Jehovah is my strength and my song;" "therefore with joy shall ye draw water out of the wells of salvation." Isa. 12:2, 3.

As the sons of Joseph made preparation to attend the Feast of Tabernacles, they saw that Christ made no movement signifying His intention of attending. They watched Him with anxiety. Since the healing at Bethesda He had not attended the national gatherings. To avoid useless conflict with the leaders at Jerusalem, He had restricted His labors to Galilee. His apparent neglect of the great religious assemblies, and the enmity manifested toward Him by the priests and rabbis, were a cause of perplexity to the people about Him, and even to His own disciples and His kindred. In His teachings He had dwelt upon the blessings of obedience to the law of God, and yet He Himself seemed to be indifferent to the service which had been divinely established. His mingling with publicans and others of ill repute, His disregard of the rabbinical observances, and the freedom with which He set aside the traditional requirements concerning the Sabbath, all seeming to place Him in antagonism to the religious authorities, excited much questioning. His brothers thought it a mistake for Him to alienate the great and learned men of the nation. They felt that these men must be in the right, and that Jesus was at fault in placing Himself in antagonism to them. But they had witnessed His blameless life, and though they did not rank themselves with His disciples, they had been deeply impressed by His works. His popularity in Galilee was gratifying to their ambition; they still hoped that He would give an evidence of His power which would lead the Pharisees to see that He was what He claimed to be. What if He were the Messiah, the Prince of Israel! They cherished this thought with proud satisfaction.

So anxious were they about this that they urged Christ to go to Jerusalem. "Depart hence," they said, "and go into Judea, that Thy disciples also may see the works that Thou doest. For there is no man that doeth anything in secret, and he himself seeketh to be known openly. If Thou do these things, show Thyself to the world." The "if" expressed doubt and unbelief. They attributed cowardice and weakness to Him. If He knew that He was the Messiah, why this strange reserve and inaction? If He really possessed such power, why not go boldly to Jerusalem, and assert His claims? Why not perform in Jerusalem the wonderful works reported of Him in Galilee? Do not hide in secluded provinces, they said, and perform your mighty works for the benefit of ignorant peasants and fishermen. Present yourself at the capital, win the support of the priests and rulers, and unite the nation in establishing the new kingdom.

These brothers of Jesus reasoned from the selfish motive so often found in the hearts of those ambitious for display. This spirit was the ruling spirit of the world. They were offended because, instead of seeking a temporal throne, Christ had declared Himself to be the bread of life. They were greatly disappointed when so many of His disciples forsook Him. They themselves turned from Him to escape the cross of acknowledging what His works revealed—that He was the Sent of God.

"Then Jesus said unto them, My time is not yet come: but your time is alway ready. The world cannot hate you; but Me it hateth, because I testify of it, that the works thereof are evil. Go ye up unto this feast: I go not up yet unto this feast; for My time is not yet full come. When He had said these words unto them, He abode still in Galilee." His brothers had spoken to Him in a tone of authority, prescribing the course He should pursue. He cast their rebuke back to them, classing them not with His self-denying disciples, but with the world. "The world cannot hate you," He said, "but Me it hateth, because I testify of it, that the works thereof are evil." The world does not hate those who are like it in spirit; it loves them as its own.

The world for Christ was not a place of ease and self-aggrandizement. He was not watching for an opportunity to seize its power and its glory. It held out no such prize for Him. It was the place into which His Father had sent Him. He had been given for the life of the world, to work out the great plan of redemption. He was accomplishing His work for the fallen race. But He was not to be presumptuous, not to rush into danger, not to hasten a crisis. Each event in His work had its appointed hour. He must wait patiently. He knew that He was to receive the world's hatred; He knew that His work would result in His death; but to prematurely expose Himself would not be the will of His Father.

From Jerusalem the report of Christ's miracles had spread wherever the Jews were dispersed; and although for many months He had been absent from the feasts, the interest in Him had not abated. Many from all parts of the world had come up to the Feast of Tabernacles in the hope of seeing Him. At the beginning of the feast many inquiries were made for Him. The Pharisees and rulers looked for Him to come, hoping for an opportunity to condemn Him. They anxiously inquired, "Where is He?" but no one knew. The thought of Him was uppermost in all minds. Through fear of the priests and rulers, none dared acknowledge Him as the Messiah, but everywhere there was quiet yet earnest discussion concerning Him. Many defended Him as one sent from God, while others denounced Him as a deceiver of the people.

Meanwhile Jesus had quietly arrived at Jerusalem. He had chosen an unfrequented route by which to go, in order to avoid the travelers who were making their way to the city from all quarters. Had He joined any of the caravans that went up to the feast, public attention would have been attracted to Him on His entrance into the city, and a popular demonstration in His favor would have aroused the authorities against Him. It was to avoid this that He chose to make the journey alone.

In the midst of the feast, when the excitement concerning Him was at its height, He entered the court of the temple in the presence of the multitude. Because of His absence from the feast, it had been urged that He dared not place Himself in the power of the priests and rulers. All were surprised at His presence. Every voice was hushed. All wondered at the dignity and courage of His bearing in the midst of powerful enemies who were thirsting for His life.

Standing thus, the center of attraction to that vast throng, Jesus addressed them as no man had ever done. His words showed a knowledge of the laws and institutions of Israel, of the sacrificial service and the teachings of the prophets, far exceeding that of the priests and rabbis. He broke through the barriers of formalism and tradition. The scenes of the future life seemed outspread before Him. As one who beheld the Unseen, He spoke of the earthly and the heavenly, the human and the divine, with positive authority. His words were most clear and convincing; and again, as at Capernaum, the people were astonished at His teaching; "for His word was with power." Luke 4:32. Under a variety of representations He warned His hearers of the calamity that would follow all who rejected the blessings He came to bring them. He had given them every possible proof that He came forth from God, and made every possible effort to bring them to repentance. He would not be rejected and murdered by His own nation if He could save them from the guilt of such a deed.

All wondered at His knowledge of the law and the prophecies; and the question passed from one to another, "How knoweth this Man letters, having never learned?" No one was regarded as qualified to be a religious teacher unless he had studied in the rabbinical schools, and both Jesus and John the Baptist had been represented as ignorant because they had not received this training. Those who heard them were astonished at their knowledge of the Scriptures, "having never learned." Of men they had not, truly; but the God of heaven was their teacher, and from Him they had received the highest kind of wisdom.

As Jesus spoke in the temple court, the people were held spellbound. The very men who were the most violent against Him felt themselves powerless to do Him harm. For the time, all other interests were forgotten.

Day after day He taught the people, until the last, "that great day of the feast." The morning of this day found the people wearied from the long season of festivity. Suddenly Jesus lifted up His voice, in tones that rang through the courts of the temple:

"If any man thirst, let him come unto Me, and drink. He that believeth on Me, as the scripture hath said, out of his belly shall flow rivers of living water." The condition of the people made this appeal very forcible. They had been engaged in a continued scene of pomp and festivity, their eyes had been dazzled with light and color, and their ears regaled with the richest music; but there had been nothing in all this round of ceremonies to meet the wants of the spirit, nothing to satisfy the thirst of the soul for that which perishes not. Jesus invited them to come and drink of the fountain of life, of that which would be in them a well of water, springing up unto everlasting life.

The priest had that morning performed the ceremony which commemorated the smiting of the rock in the wilderness. That rock was a symbol of Him who by His death would cause living streams of salvation to flow to all who are athirst. Christ's words were the water of life. There in the presence of the assembled multitude He set Himself apart to be smitten, that the water of life might flow to the world. In smiting Christ, Satan thought to destroy the Prince of life; but from the smitten rock there flowed living water. As Jesus thus spoke to the people, their hearts thrilled with a strange awe, and many were ready to exclaim, with the woman of Samaria, "Give me this water, that I thirst not." John 4:15.

Jesus knew the wants of the soul. Pomp, riches, and honor cannot satisfy the heart. "If any man thirst, let him come unto Me." The rich, the poor, the high, the low, are alike welcome. He promises to relieve the burdened mind, to comfort the sorrowing, and to give hope to the despondent. Many of those who heard Jesus were mourners over disappointed hopes, many were nourishing a secret grief, many were seeking to satisfy their restless longing with the things of the world and the praise of men; but when all was gained, they found that they had toiled only to reach a broken cistern, from which they could not quench their thirst. Amid the glitter of the joyous scene they stood, dissatisfied and sad. That sudden cry, "If any man thirst," startled them from their sorrowful meditation, and as they listened to the words that followed, their minds kindled with a new hope. The Holy Spirit presented the symbol before them until they saw in it the offer of the priceless gift of salvation.

The cry of Christ to the thirsty soul is still going forth, and it appeals to us with even greater power than to those who heard it in the temple on that last day of the feast. The fountain is open for all. The weary and exhausted ones are offered the refreshing draught of eternal life. Jesus is still crying, "If any man thirst, let him come unto Me, and drink." "Let him that is athirst come. And whosoever will, let him take the water of life freely." "Whosoever drinketh of the water that I shall give him shall never thirst; but the water that I shall give him shall be in him a well of water springing up into everlasting life." Rev. 22:17; John 4:14.

11

Among Snares

This chapter is based on John 7:16-36; 40-53; 8:1-11.

A ll the while Jesus was at Jerusalem during the feast He was shadowed by spies. Day after day new schemes to silence Him were tried. The priests and rulers were watching to entrap Him. They were planning to stop Him by violence. But this was not all. They wanted to humble this Galilean rabbi before the people.

On the first day of His presence at the feast, the rulers had come to Him, demanding by what authority He taught. They wished to divert attention from Him to the question of His right to teach, and thus to their own importance and authority.

"My teaching is not Mine," said Jesus, "but His that sent Me. If any man willeth to do His will, he shall know of the teaching, whether it be of God, or whether I speak from Myself." John 7:16, 17, R. V. The question of these cavilers Jesus met, not by answering the cavil, but by opening up truth vital to the salvation of the soul. The perception and appreciation of truth, He said, depends less upon the mind than upon the heart. Truth must be received into the soul; it claims the homage of the will. If truth could be submitted to the reason alone, pride would be no hindrance in the way of its reception. But it is to be received through the work of grace in the heart; and its reception depends upon the renunciation of every sin that the Spirit of God reveals. Man's advantages for obtaining a knowledge of the truth, however great these may be, will prove of no benefit to him unless the heart is open to receive the truth, and there is a conscientious surrender of every habit and practice that is opposed to its principles. To those who thus yield themselves to God, having an honest desire to know and to do His will, the truth is revealed as the power of God for their salvation. These will be able to distinguish between him who speaks for God, and him who speaks merely from himself. The Pharisees had not put their will on the side of God's will. They were not seeking to know the truth, but to find some excuse for evading it; Christ showed that this was why they did not understand His teaching.

He now gave a test by which the true teacher might be distinguished from the deceiver: "He that speaketh from himself seeketh his own glory: but he that seeketh the glory of Him that sent him, the same is true, and no unrighteousness is in him." John 7:18, R. V. He that seeketh his own glory is speaking only from himself. The spirit of self-seeking betrays its origin. But Christ was seeking the glory of God. He spoke the words of God. This was the evidence of His authority as a teacher of the truth.

Jesus gave the rabbis an evidence of His divinity by showing that He read their hearts. Ever since the healing at Bethesda they had been plotting His death. Thus they were themselves breaking the law which they professed to be defending. "Did not Moses give you the law," He said, "and yet none of you keepeth the law? Why go ye about to kill Me?"

Like a swift flash of light these words revealed to the rabbis the pit of ruin into which they were about to plunge. For an instant they were filled with terror. They saw that they were in conflict with Infinite Power. But they would not be warned. In order to maintain their influence with the people, their murderous designs must be concealed. Evading the question of Jesus, they exclaimed, "Thou hast a devil: who goeth about to kill Thee?" They insinuated that the wonderful works of Jesus were instigated by an evil spirit.

To this insinuation Christ gave no heed. He went on to show that His work of healing at Bethesda was in harmony with the Sabbath law, and that it was justified by the interpretation which the Jews themselves put upon the law. He said, "Moses therefore gave unto you circumcision; . . . and ye on the Sabbath day circumcise a man." According to the law, every child must be circumcised on the eighth day. Should the appointed time fall upon the Sabbath, the rite must then be performed. How much more must it be in harmony with the spirit of the law to make a man "every whit whole on the Sabbath day." And He warned them to "judge not according to the appearance, but judge righteous judgment."

The rulers were silenced; and many of the people exclaimed, "Is not this He, whom they seek to kill? But, lo, He speaketh boldly, and they say nothing unto Him. Do the rulers know indeed that this is the very Christ?"

Many among Christ's hearers who were dwellers at Jerusalem, and who were not ignorant of the plots of the rulers against Him, felt themselves drawn to Him by an irresistible power. The conviction pressed upon them that He was the Son of God. But Satan was ready to suggest doubt; and for this the way was prepared by their own erroneous ideas of the Messiah and His coming. It was generally believed that Christ would be born at Bethlehem, but that after a time He would disappear, and at His second appearance none would know whence He came. There were not a few who held that the Messiah would have no natural relationship to humanity. And because the popular conception of the glory of the Messiah was not met by Jesus of Nazareth, many gave heed to the suggestion, "Howbeit we know this Man whence He is: but when Christ cometh, no man knoweth whence He is."

While they were thus wavering between doubt and faith, Jesus took up their thoughts and answered them: "Ye both know Me, and ye know whence I am: and I am not come of Myself, but He that sent Me is true, whom ye know not." They claimed a knowledge of what the origin of Christ should be, but they were in utter ignorance of it. If they had lived in accordance with the will of God, they would have known His Son when He was manifested to them.

The hearers could not but understand Christ's words. Clearly they were a repetition of the claim He had made in the presence of the Sanhedrin many months before, when He declared Himself the Son of God. As the rulers then tried to compass His death, so now they sought to take Him; but they were prevented by an unseen power, which put a limit to their rage, saying to them, Thus far shalt thou go, and no farther.

Among the people many believed on Him, and they said, "When Christ cometh, will He do more miracles than these which this Man hath done?" The leaders of the Pharisees, who were anxiously watching the course of events, caught the expressions of sympathy among the throng. Hurrying away to the chief priests, they laid their plans to arrest Him. They arranged, however, to take Him when He was alone; for they dared not seize Him in the presence of the people. Again Jesus made it manifest that He read their purpose. "Yet a little while am I with you," He said, "and then I go unto Him that sent Me. Ye shall seek Me, and shall not find Me: and where I am, thither ye cannot come." Soon He would find a refuge beyond the reach of their scorn and hate. He would ascend to the Father, to be again the Adored of the angels; and thither His murderers could never come.

Sneeringly the rabbis said, "Whither will He go, that we shall not find Him? will He go unto the dispersed among the Gentiles, and teach the Gentiles?" Little did these cavilers dream that in their mocking words they were picturing the mission of the Christ! All day long He had stretched forth His hands unto a disobedient and gainsaying people; yet He would be found of them that sought Him not; among a people that had not called upon His name He would be manifest. Rom. 10:20, 21.

Many who were convinced that Jesus was the Son of God were misled by the false reasoning of the priests and rabbis. These teachers had repeated with great effect the prophecies concerning the Messiah, that He would "reign in Mount Zion, and in Jerusalem, and before His ancients gloriously;" that He would "have dominion also from sea to sea, and from the river unto the ends of the earth." Isa. 24:23; Ps. 72:8. Then they made contemptuous comparisons between the glory here pictured and the humble appearance of Jesus. The very words of prophecy were so perverted as to sanction error. Had the people in sincerity studied the word for themselves, they would not have been misled. The sixty-first chapter of Isaiah testifies that Christ was to do the very work He did. Chapter fifty-three sets forth His rejection and sufferings in the world, and chapter fifty-nine describes the character of the priests and rabbis.

God does not compel men to give up their unbelief. Before them are light and darkness, truth and error. It is for them to decide which they will accept. The human mind is endowed with power to discriminate between right and wrong. God designs that men shall not decide from impulse, but from weight of evidence, carefully comparing scripture with scripture. Had the Jews laid by their prejudice and compared written prophecy with the facts characterizing the life of Jesus, they would have perceived a beautiful harmony between the prophecies and their fulfillment in the life and ministry of the lowly Galilean.

Many are deceived today in the same way as were the Jews. Religious teachers read the Bible in the light of their own understanding and traditions; and the people do not search the Scriptures for themselves, and judge for themselves as to what is truth; but they yield up their judgment, and commit their souls to their leaders. The preaching and teaching of His word is one of the means that God has ordained for diffusing light; but we must bring every man's teaching to the test of Scripture. Whoever will prayerfully study the Bible, desiring to know the truth, that he may obey it, will receive divine enlightenment. He will understand the Scriptures. "If any man willeth to do His will, he shall know of the teaching." John 7:17, R. V.

On the last day of the feast, the officers sent out by the priests and rulers to arrest Jesus, returned without Him. They were angrily questioned, "Why have ye not brought Him?" With solemn countenance they answered, "Never man spake like this Man."

Hardened as were their hearts, they were melted by His words. While He was speaking in the temple court, they had lingered near, to catch something that might be turned against Him. But as they listened, the purpose for which they had been sent was forgotten. They stood as men entranced. Christ revealed Himself to their souls. They saw that which priests and rulers would not see,—humanity flooded with the glory of divinity. They returned, so filled with this thought, so impressed by His words, that to the inquiry, "Why have ye not brought Him?" they could only reply, "Never man spake like this Man."

The priests and rulers, on first coming into the presence of Christ, had felt the same conviction. Their hearts were deeply moved, and the thought was forced upon them, "Never man spake like this Man." But they had stifled the conviction of the Holy Spirit. Now, enraged that even the instruments of the law should be influenced by the hated Galilean, they cried, "Are ye also deceived? Have any of the rulers or of the Pharisees believed on Him? But this people who knoweth not the law are cursed."

Those to whom the message of truth is spoken seldom ask, "Is it true?" but, "By whom is it advocated?" Multitudes estimate it by the numbers who accept it; and the question is still asked, "Have any of the learned men or religious leaders believed?" Men are no more favorable to real godliness now than in the days of Christ. They are just as intently seeking earthly good, to the neglect of eternal riches; and it is not an argument against the truth, that large numbers are not ready to accept it, or that it is not received by the world's great men, or even by the religious leaders.

Again the priests and rulers proceeded to lay plans for arresting Jesus. It was urged that if He were longer left at liberty, He would draw the people away from the established leaders, and the only safe course was to silence Him without delay. In the full tide of their discussion, they were suddenly checked. Nicodemus questioned, "Doth our law judge any man, before it hear him, and know what he doeth?" Silence fell on the assembly. The words of Nicodemus came home to their consciences. They could not condemn a man unheard. But it was not for this reason alone that the haughty rulers remained silent, gazing at him who had dared to speak in favor of justice. They were startled and chagrined that one of their own number had been so far impressed by the character of Jesus as to speak a word in His defense. Recovering from their astonishment, they addressed Nicodemus with cutting sarcasm, "Art thou also of Galilee? Search and look: for out of Galilee ariseth no prophet."

Yet the protest resulted in staying the proceedings of the council. The rulers were unable to carry out their purpose and condemn Jesus without a hearing. Defeated for the time, "every man went unto his own house. Jesus went unto the Mount of Olives."

From the excitement and confusion of the city, from the eager crowds and the treacherous rabbis, Jesus turned away to the quiet of the olive groves, where He could be alone with God. But in the early morning He returned to the temple, and as the people gathered about Him, He sat down and taught them.

He was soon interrupted. A group of Pharisees and scribes approached Him, dragging with them a terror-stricken woman, whom with hard, eager voices they accused of having violated the seventh commandment. Having pushed her into the presence of Jesus, they said to Him, with a hypocritical show of respect, "Moses in the law commanded us, that such should be stoned: but what sayest Thou?"

Their pretended reverence veiled a deep-laid plot for His ruin. They had seized upon this opportunity to secure His condemnation, thinking that whatever decision He might make, they would find occasion to accuse Him. Should He acquit the woman, He might be charged with despising the law of Moses. Should He declare her worthy of death, He could be accused to the Romans as one who was assuming authority that belonged only to them.

Jesus looked for a moment upon the scene,—the trembling victim in her shame, the hard-faced dignitaries, devoid of even human pity. His spirit of stainless purity shrank from the spectacle. Well He knew for what purpose this case had been brought to Him. He read the heart, and knew the character and life history of everyone in His presence. These would-be guardians of justice had themselves led their victim into sin, that they might lay a snare for Jesus. Giving no sign that He had heard their question, He stooped, and fixing His eyes upon the ground, began to write in the dust.

Impatient at His delay and apparent indifference, the accusers drew nearer, urging the matter upon His attention. But as their eyes, following those of Jesus, fell upon the pavement at His feet, their countenances changed. There, traced before them, were the guilty secrets of their own lives. The people, looking on, saw the sudden change of expression, and pressed forward to discover what it was that they were regarding with such astonishment and shame.

With all their professions of reverence for the law, these rabbis, in bringing the charge against the woman, were disregarding its provisions. It was the husband's duty to take action against her, and the guilty parties were to be punished equally. The action of the accusers was wholly unauthorized. Jesus, however, met them on their own ground. The law specified that in punishment by stoning, the witnesses in the case should be the first to cast a stone. Now rising, and fixing His eyes upon the plotting elders, Jesus said, "He that is without sin among you, let him first cast a stone at her." And stooping down, He continued writing on the ground.

He had not set aside the law given through Moses, nor infringed upon the authority of Rome. The accusers had been defeated. Now, their robe of pretended holiness torn from them, they stood, guilty and condemned, in the presence of Infinite Purity. They trembled lest the hidden iniquity of their lives should be laid open to the multitude; and one by one, with bowed heads and downcast eyes, they stole away, leaving their victim with the pitying Saviour.

Jesus arose, and looking at the woman said, "Woman, where are those thine accusers? hath no man condemned thee? She said, No man, Lord. And Jesus said unto her, Neither do I condemn thee: go, and sin no more."

The woman had stood before Jesus, cowering with fear. His words, "He that is without sin among you, let him first cast a stone," had come to her as a death sentence. She dared not lift her eyes to the Saviour's face, but silently awaited her doom. In astonishment she saw her accusers depart speechless and confounded; then those words of hope fell upon her ear, "Neither do I condemn thee: go, and sin no more." Her heart was melted, and she cast herself at the feet of Jesus, sobbing out her grateful love, and with bitter tears confessing her sins.

This was to her the beginning of a new life, a life of purity and peace, devoted to the service of God. In the uplifting of this fallen soul, Jesus performed a greater miracle than in healing the most grievous physical disease; He cured the spiritual malady which is unto death everlasting. This penitent woman became one of His most steadfast followers. With self-sacrificing love and devotion she repaid His forgiving mercy.

In His act of pardoning this woman and encouraging her to live a better life, the character of Jesus shines forth in the beauty of perfect righteousness. While He does not palliate sin, nor lessen the sense of guilt, He seeks not to condemn, but to save. The world had for this erring woman only contempt and scorn; but Jesus speaks words of comfort and hope. The Sinless One pities the weakness of the sinner, and reaches to her a helping hand. While the hypocritical Pharisees denounce, Jesus bids her, "Go, and sin no more."

It is not Christ's follower that, with averted eyes, turns from the erring, leaving them unhindered to pursue their downward course. Those who are forward in accusing others, and zealous in bringing them to justice, are often in their own lives more guilty than they. Men hate the sinner, while they love the sin. Christ hates the sin, but loves the sinner. This will be the spirit of all who follow Him. Christian love is slow to censure, quick to discern penitence, ready to forgive, to encourage, to set the wanderer in the path of holiness, and to stay his feet therein.

12

"The Light of Life"

This chapter is based on John 8:12-59; 9.

Then spake Jesus again unto them, saying, I am the light of the world: he that followeth Me shall not walk in darkness, but shall have the light of life."

When He spoke these words, Jesus was in the court of the temple specially connected with the services of the Feast of Tabernacles. In the center of this court rose two lofty standards, supporting lampstands of great size. After the evening sacrifice, all the lamps were kindled, shedding their light over Jerusalem. This ceremony was in commemoration of the pillar of light that guided Israel in the desert, and was also regarded as pointing to the coming of the Messiah. At evening when the lamps were lighted, the court was a scene of great rejoicing. Gray-haired men, the priests of the temple and the rulers of the people, united in the festive dances to the sound of instrumental music and the chants of the Levites.

In the illumination of Jerusalem, the people expressed their hope of the Messiah's coming to shed His light upon Israel. But to Jesus the scene had a wider meaning. As the radiant lamps of the temple lighted up all about them, so Christ, the source of spiritual light, illumines the darkness of the world. Yet the symbol was imperfect. That great light which His own hand had set in the heavens was a truer representation of the glory of His mission.

It was morning; the sun had just risen above the Mount of Olives, and its rays fell with dazzling brightness on the marble palaces, and lighted up the gold of the temple walls, when Jesus, pointing to it, said, "I am the light of the world."

By one who listened to these words, they were long afterward re-echoed in that sublime passage, "In Him was life; and the life was the light of men. And the light shineth in the darkness; and the darkness apprehended it not." "That was the true light, which lighteth every man that cometh into the world." John 1:4, 5, R. V., 9. And long after Jesus had ascended to heaven, Peter also, writing under the illumination of the divine Spirit, recalled the symbol Christ had used: "We have also a more sure word of prophecy; whereunto ye do well that ye take heed, as unto a light that shineth in a dark place, until the day dawn, and the daystar arise in your hearts." 2 Peter 1:19.

In the manifestation of God to His people, light had ever been a symbol of His presence. At the creative word in the beginning, light had shone out of darkness. Light had been enshrouded in the pillar of cloud by day and the pillar of fire by night, leading the vast armies of Israel. Light blazed with awful grandeur about the Lord on Mount Sinai. Light rested over the mercy seat in the tabernacle. Light filled the temple of Solomon at its dedication. Light shone on the hills of Bethlehem when the angels brought the message of redemption to the watching shepherds.

God is light; and in the words, "I am the light of the world," Christ declared His oneness with God, and His relation to the whole human family. It was He who at the beginning had caused "the light to shine out of darkness." 2 Cor. 4:6. He is the light of sun and moon and star. He was the spiritual light that in symbol and type and prophecy had shone upon Israel. But not to the Jewish nation alone was the light given. As the sunbeams penetrate to the remotest corners of the earth, so does the light of the Sun of Righteousness shine upon every soul.

"That was the true light, which lighteth every man that cometh into the world." The world has had its great teachers, men of giant intellect and wonderful research, men whose utterances have stimulated thought, and opened to view vast fields of knowledge; and these men have been honored as guides and benefactors of their race. But there is One who stands higher than they. "As many as received Him, to them gave He power to become the sons of God." "No man hath seen God at any time; the only-begotten Son, which is in the bosom of the Father, He hath declared Him." John 1:12, 18. We can trace the line of the world's great teachers as far back as human records extend; but the Light was before them. As the moon and the stars of the solar system shine by the reflected light of the sun, so, as far as their teaching is true, do the world's great thinkers reflect the rays of the Sun of Righteousness. Every gem of thought, every flash of the intellect, is from the Light of the world. In these days we hear much about "higher education." The true "higher education" is that imparted by Him "in whom are hid all the treasures of wisdom and knowledge." "In Him was life; and the life was the light of men." Col. 2:3; John 1:4. "He that followeth Me," said Jesus, "shall not walk in darkness, but shall have the light of life."

In the words, "I am the light of the world," Jesus declared Himself the Messiah. The aged Simeon, in the temple where Christ was now teaching, had spoken of Him as "a light to lighten the Gentiles, and the glory of Thy people Israel." Luke 2:32. In these words he was applying to Him a prophecy familiar to all Israel. By the prophet Isaiah, the Holy Spirit had declared, "It is too light a thing that Thou shouldest be My servant to raise up the tribes of Jacob, and to restore the preserved of Israel: I will also give Thee for a light to the Gentiles, that Thou mayest be My salvation unto the end of the earth." Isa. 49:6, R. V. This prophecy was generally understood as spoken of the Messiah, and when Jesus said, "I am the light of the world," the people could not fail to recognize His claim to be the Promised One.

To the Pharisees and rulers this claim seemed an arrogant assumption. That a man like themselves should make such pretensions they could not tolerate. Seeming to ignore His words, they demanded, "Who art Thou?" They were bent upon forcing Him to declare Himself the Christ. His appearance and His work were so at variance with the expectations of the people, that, as His wily enemies believed, a direct announcement of Himself as the Messiah would cause Him to be rejected as an impostor.

But to their question, "Who art Thou?" Jesus replied, "Even that which I have also spoken unto you from the beginning." John 8:25, R.V. That which had been revealed in His words was revealed also in His character. He was the embodiment of the truths He taught. "I do nothing of Myself," He continued; "but as My Father hath taught Me, I speak these things. And He that sent Me is with Me: the Father hath not left Me alone; for I do always those things that please Him." He did not attempt to prove His Messianic claim, but showed His unity with God. If their minds had been open to God's love, they would have received Jesus.

Among His hearers many were drawn to Him in faith, and to them He said, "if ye continue in My word, then are ye My disciples indeed; and ye shall know the truth, and the truth shall make you free."

These words offended the Pharisees. The nation's long subjection to a foreign yoke, they disregarded, and angrily exclaimed, "We be Abraham's seed, and were never in bondage to any man: how sayest Thou, Ye shall be made free?" Jesus looked upon these men, the slaves of malice, whose thoughts were bent upon revenge, and sadly answered, "Verily, verily, I say unto you, Whosoever committeth sin is the servant of sin." They were in the worst kind of bondage,—ruled by the spirit of evil.

Every soul that refuses to give himself to God is under the control of another power. He is not his own. He may talk of freedom, but he is in the most abject slavery. He is not allowed to see the beauty of truth, for his mind is under the control of Satan. While he flatters himself that he is following the dictates of his own judgment, he obeys the will of the prince of darkness. Christ came to break the shackles of sin-slavery from the soul. "If the Son therefore shall make you free, ye shall be free indeed." "The law of the Spirit of life in Christ Jesus" sets us "free from the law of sin and death." Rom. 8:2.

In the work of redemption there is no compulsion. No external force is employed. Under the influence of the Spirit of God, man is left free to choose whom he will serve. In the change that takes place when the soul surrenders to Christ, there is the highest sense of freedom. The expulsion of sin is the act of the soul itself. True, we have no power to free ourselves from Satan's control; but when we desire to be set free from sin, and in our great need cry out for a power out of and above ourselves, the powers of the soul are imbued with the divine energy of the Holy Spirit, and they obey the dictates of the will in fulfilling the will of God.

The only condition upon which the freedom of man is possible is that of becoming one with Christ. "The truth shall make you free;" and Christ is the truth. Sin can triumph only by enfeebling the mind, and destroying the liberty of the soul. Subjection to God is restoration to one's self,—to the true glory and dignity of man. The divine law, to which we are brought into subjection, is "the law of liberty." James 2:12.

The Pharisees had declared themselves the children of Abraham. Jesus told them that this claim could be established only by doing the works of Abraham. The true children of Abraham would live, as he did, a life of obedience to God. They would not try to kill One who was speaking the truth that was given Him from God. In plotting against Christ, the rabbis were not doing the works of Abraham. A mere lineal descent from Abraham was of no value. Without a spiritual connection with him, which would be manifested in possessing the same spirit, and doing the same works, they were not his children.

This principle bears with equal weight upon a question that has long agitated the Christian world,—the question of apostolic succession. Descent from Abraham was proved, not by name and lineage, but by likeness of character. So the apostolic succession rests not upon the transmission of ecclesiastical authority, but upon spiritual relationship. A life actuated by the apostles' spirit, the belief and teaching of the truth they taught, this is the true evidence of apostolic succession. This is what constitutes men the successors of the first teachers of the gospel.

Jesus denied that the Jews were children of Abraham. He said, "Ye do the deeds of your father." In mockery they answered, "*We* be not born of fornication; we have one Father, even God." These words, in allusion to the circumstances of His birth, were intended as a thrust against Christ in the presence of those who were beginning to believe on Him. Jesus gave no heed to the base insinuation, but said, "If God were your Father, ye would love Me: for I proceeded forth and came from God."

Their works testified of their relationship to him who was a liar and a murderer. "Ye are of your father the devil," said Jesus, "and the lusts of your father it is your will to do. He was a murderer from the beginning, and stood not in the truth, because there is no truth in him. . . . Because I say the truth, ye believe Me not." John 8:44, 45, R. V. The fact that Jesus spoke the truth, and that with certainty, was why He was not received by the Jewish leaders. It was the truth that offended these self-righteous men. The truth exposed the fallacy of error; it condemned their teaching and practice, and it was unwelcome. They would rather close their eyes to the truth than humble themselves to confess that they had been in error. They did not love the truth. They did not desire it, even though it was truth.

"Which of you convicteth [Revised Version] Me of sin? And if I say the truth, why do ye not believe Me?" Day by day for three years His enemies had been following Christ, trying to find some stain in His character. Satan and all the confederacy of evil had been seeking to overcome Him; but they had found nothing in Him by which to gain an advantage. Even the devils were forced to confess, "Thou art the Holy One of God." Mark 1:24. Jesus lived the law in the sight of heaven, in the sight of unfallen worlds, and in the sight of sinful men. Before angels, men, and demons, He had spoken, unchallenged, words that from any other lips would have been blasphemy: "I do always those things that please Him."

The fact that although they could find no sin in Christ the Jews would not receive Him proved that they themselves had no connection with God. They did not recognize His voice in the message of His Son. They thought themselves passing judgment on Christ; but in rejecting Him they were pronouncing sentence upon themselves. "He that is of God," said Jesus, "heareth God's words: ye therefore hear them not, because ye are not of God."

The lesson is true for all time. Many a man who delights to quibble, to criticize, seeking for something to question in the word of God, thinks that he is thereby giving evidence of independence of thought, and mental acuteness. He supposes that he is sitting in judgment on the Bible, when in truth he is judging himself. He makes it manifest that he is incapable of appreciating truths that originate in heaven, and that compass eternity. In presence of the great mountain of God's righteousness, his spirit is not awed. He busies himself with hunting for sticks and straws, and in this betrays a narrow and earthly nature, a heart that is fast losing its capacity to appreciate God. He whose heart has responded to the divine touch will be seeking for that which will increase his knowledge of God, and will refine and elevate the character. As a flower turns to the sun, that the bright rays may touch it with tints of beauty, so will the soul turn to the Sun of Righteousness, that heaven's light may beautify the character with the graces of the character of Christ.

Jesus continued, drawing a sharp contrast between the position of the Jews and that of Abraham: "Your father Abraham rejoiced to see My day: and he saw it, and was glad."

Abraham had greatly desired to see the promised Saviour. He offered up the most earnest prayer that before his death he might behold the Messiah. And he saw Christ. A supernatural light was given him, and he acknowledged Christ's divine character. He saw His day, and was glad. He was given a view of the divine sacrifice for sin. Of this sacrifice he had an illustration in his own experience. The command came to him, "Take now thy son, thine only son Isaac, whom thou lovest, . . . and offer him . . . for a burnt offering." Gen. 22:2. Upon the altar of sacrifice he laid the son of promise, the son in whom his hopes were centered. Then as he waited beside the altar with knife upraised to obey God, he heard a voice from heaven saying, "Lay not thine hand upon the lad, neither do thou anything unto him: for now I know that thou fearest God, seeing thou hast not withheld thy son, thine only son from Me." Gen. 22:12. This terrible ordeal was imposed upon Abraham that he might see the day of Christ, and realize the great love of God for the world, so great that to raise it from its degradation, He gave His only-begotten Son to a most shameful death.

Abraham learned of God the greatest lesson ever given to mortal. His prayer that he might see Christ before he should die was answered. He saw Christ; he saw all that mortal can see, and live. By making an entire surrender, he was able to understand the vision of Christ, which had been given him. He was shown that in giving His only-begotten Son to save sinners from eternal ruin, God was making a greater and more wonderful sacrifice than ever man could make.

Abraham's experience answered the question: "Wherewith shall I come before the Lord, and bow myself before the high God? Shall I come before Him with burnt offerings, with calves of a year old? Will the Lord be pleased with thousands of rams, or with ten thousands of rivers of oil? shall I give my first-born for my transgression, the fruit of my body for the sin of my soul?" Micah 6:6, 7. In the words of Abraham, "My son, God will provide Himself a lamb for a burnt offering," (Gen. 22:8), and in God's provision of a sacrifice instead of Isaac, it was declared that no man could make expiation for himself. The pagan system of sacrifice was wholly unacceptable to God. No father was to offer up his son or his daughter for a sin offering. The Son of God alone can bear the guilt of the world.

Through his own suffering, Abraham was enabled to behold the Saviour's mission of sacrifice. But Israel would not understand that which was so unwelcome to their proud hearts. Christ's words concerning Abraham conveyed to His hearers no deep significance. The Pharisees saw in them only fresh ground for caviling. They retorted with a sneer, as if they would prove Jesus to be a madman, "Thou art not yet fifty years old, and hast Thou seen Abraham?"

With solemn dignity Jesus answered, "Verily, verily, I say unto you, Before Abraham was, I Am."

Silence fell upon the vast assembly. The name of God, given to Moses to express the idea of the eternal presence, had been claimed as His own by this Galilean Rabbi. He had announced Himself to be the self-existent One, He who had been promised to Israel, "whose goings forth have been from of old, from the days of eternity." Micah 5:2, margin.

Again the priests and rabbis cried out against Jesus as a blasphemer. His claim to be one with God had before stirred them to take His life, and a few months later they plainly declared, "For a good work we stone Thee not; but for blasphemy; and because that Thou, being a man, makest Thyself God." John 10:33. Because He was, and avowed Himself to be, the Son of God, they were bent on destroying Him. Now many of the people, siding with the priests and rabbis, took up stones to cast at Him. "But Jesus hid Himself, and went out of the temple, going through the midst of them, and so passed by."

The Light was shining in darkness; but "the darkness apprehended it not." John 1:5, R. V.

"As Jesus passed by, He saw a man which was blind from his birth. And His disciples asked Him, saying, Master, who did sin, this man, or his parents, that he was born blind? Jesus answered, Neither hath this man sinned, nor his parents: but that the works of God should be made manifest in him. . . . When He had thus spoken, He spat on the ground, and made clay of the spittle, and He anointed the eyes of the blind man with the clay, and said unto him, Go, wash in the pool of Siloam, (which is by interpretation, Sent). He went his way therefore, and washed, and came seeing."

It was generally believed by the Jews that sin is punished in this life. Every affliction was regarded as the penalty of some wrongdoing, either of the sufferer himself or of his parents. It is true that all suffering results from the transgression of God's law, but this truth had become perverted. Satan, the author of sin and all its results, had led men to look upon disease and death as proceeding from God,—as punishment arbitrarily inflicted on account of sin. Hence one upon whom some great affliction or calamity had fallen had the additional burden of being regarded as a great sinner.

Thus the way was prepared for the Jews to reject Jesus. He who "hath borne our griefs, and carried our sorrows" was looked upon by the Jews as "stricken, smitten of God, and afflicted;" and they hid their faces from Him. Isa. 53:4, 3.

God had given a lesson designed to prevent this. The history of Job had shown that suffering is inflicted by Satan, and is overruled by God for purposes of mercy. But Israel did not understand the lesson. The same error for which God had reproved the friends of Job was repeated by the Jews in their rejection of Christ.

The belief of the Jews in regard to the relation of sin and suffering was held by Christ's disciples. While Jesus corrected their error, He did not explain the cause of the man's affliction, but told them what would be the result. Because of it the works of God would be made manifest. "As long as I am in the world," He said, "I am the light of the world." Then having anointed the eyes of the blind man, He sent him to wash in the pool of Siloam, and the man's sight was restored. Thus Jesus answered the question of the disciples in a practical way, as He usually answered questions put to Him from curiosity. The disciples were not called upon to discuss the question as to who had sinned or had not sinned, but to understand the power and mercy of God in giving sight to the blind. It was evident that there was no healing virtue in the clay, or in the pool wherein the blind man was sent to wash, but that the virtue was in Christ.

The Pharisees could not but be astonished at the cure. Yet they were more than ever filled with hatred; for the miracle had been performed on the Sabbath day.

The neighbors of the young man, and those who knew him before in his blindness, said, "Is not this he that sat and begged?" They looked upon him with doubt; for when his eyes were opened, his countenance was changed and brightened, and he appeared like another man. From one to another the question passed. Some said, "This is he;" others, "He is like him." But he who had received the great blessing settled the question by saying, "I am he." He then told them of Jesus, and by what means he had been healed, and they inquired, "Where is He? He said, I know not."

Then they brought him before a council of the Pharisees. Again the man was asked how he had received his sight. "He said unto them, He put clay upon mine eyes, and I washed, and do see. Therefore said some of the Pharisees, This man is not of God, because He keepeth not the Sabbath day." The Pharisees hoped to make Jesus out to be a sinner, and therefore not the Messiah. They knew not that it was He who had made the Sabbath and knew all its obligation, who had healed the blind man. They appeared wonderfully zealous for the observance of the Sabbath, yet were planning murder on that very day. But many were greatly moved at hearing of this miracle, and were convicted that He who had opened the eyes of the blind was more than a common man. In answer to the charge that Jesus was a sinner because He kept not the Sabbath day, they said, "How can a man that is a sinner do such miracles?"

Again the rabbis appealed to the blind man, "What sayest thou of Him, that He hath opened thine eyes? He said, He is a prophet." The Pharisees then asserted that he had not been born blind and received his sight. They called for his parents, and asked them, saying, "Is this your son, who ye say was born blind?"

There was the man himself, declaring that he had been blind, and had had his sight restored; but the Pharisees would rather deny the evidence of their own senses than admit that they were in error. So powerful is prejudice, so distorting is Pharisaical righteousness.

The Pharisees had one hope left, and that was to intimidate the man's parents. With apparent sincerity they asked, "How then doth he now see?" The parents feared to compromise themselves; for it had been declared that whoever should acknowledge Jesus as the Christ should be "put out of the synagogue;" that is, should be excluded from the synagogue for thirty days. During this time no child could be circumcised nor dead be lamented in the offender's home. The sentence was regarded as a great calamity; and if it failed to produce repentance, a far heavier penalty followed. The great work wrought for their son had brought conviction to the parents, yet they answered, "We know that this is our son, and that he was born blind: but by what means he now seeth, we know not; or who hath opened his eyes, we know not: he is of age; ask him: he shall speak for himself." Thus they shifted all responsibility from themselves to their son; for they dared not confess Christ.

The dilemma in which the Pharisees were placed, their questioning and prejudice, their unbelief in the facts of the case, were opening the eyes of the multitude, especially of the common people. Jesus had frequently wrought His miracles in the open street, and His work was always of a character to relieve suffering. The question in many minds was, Would God do such mighty works through an impostor, as the Pharisees insisted that Jesus was? The controversy was becoming very earnest on both sides.

The Pharisees saw that they were giving publicity to the work done by Jesus. They could not deny the miracle. The blind man was filled with joy and gratitude; he beheld the wondrous things of nature, and was filled with delight at the beauty of earth and sky. He freely related his experience, and again they tried to silence him, saying, "Give God the praise: we know that this Man is a sinner." That is, Do not say again that this Man gave you sight; it is God who has done this.

The blind man answered, "Whether He be a sinner or no, I know not: one thing I know, that, whereas I was blind, now I see."

Then they questioned again, "What did He to thee? how opened He thine eyes?" With many words they tried to confuse him, so that he might think himself deluded. Satan and his evil angels were on the side of the Pharisees, and united their energies and subtlety with man's reasoning in order to counteract the influence of Christ. They blunted the convictions that were deepening in many minds. Angels of God were also on the ground to strengthen the man who had had his sight restored.

The Pharisees did not realize that they had to deal with any other than the uneducated man who had been born blind; they knew not Him with whom they were in controversy. Divine light shone into the chambers of the blind man's soul. As these hypocrites tried to make him disbelieve, God helped him to show, by the vigor and pointedness of his replies, that he was not to be ensnared. He answered, "I have told you already, and ye did not hear: wherefore would ye hear it again? will ye also be His disciples? Then they reviled him, and said, Thou art His disciple; but we are Moses' disciples. We know that God spake unto Moses: as for this fellow, we know not from whence He is."

The Lord Jesus knew the ordeal through which the man was passing, and He gave him grace and utterance, so that he became a witness for Christ. He answered the Pharisees in words that were a cutting rebuke to his questioners. They claimed to be the expositors of Scripture, the religious guides of the nation; and yet here was One performing miracles, and they were confessedly ignorant as to the source of His power, and as to His character and claims. "Why herein is a marvelous thing," said the man, "that ye know not from whence He is, and yet He hath opened mine eyes. Now we know that God heareth not sinners: but if any man be a worshiper of God, and doeth His will, him He heareth. Since the world began was it not heard that any man opened the eyes of one that was born blind. If this Man were not of God, He could do nothing."

The man had met his inquisitors on their own ground. His reasoning was unanswerable. The Pharisees were astonished, and they held their peace,—spellbound before his pointed, determined words. For a few moments there was silence. Then the frowning priests and rabbis gathered about them their robes, as though they feared contamination from contact with him; they shook off the dust from their feet, and hurled denunciations against him,—"Thou wast altogether born in sins, and dost thou teach *us?*" And they excommunicated him.

Jesus heard what had been done; and finding him soon after, He said, "Dost thou believe on the Son of God?"

For the first time the blind man looked upon the face of his Restorer. Before the council he had seen his parents troubled and perplexed; he had looked upon the frowning faces of the rabbis; now his eyes rested upon the loving, peaceful countenance of Jesus. Already, at great cost to himself, he had acknowledged Him as a delegate of divine power; now a higher revelation was granted him.

To the Saviour's question, "Dost thou believe on the Son of God?" the blind man replied by asking, "Who is He, Lord, that I might believe on Him?" And Jesus said, "Thou hast both seen Him, and it is He that talketh with thee." The man cast himself at the Saviour's feet in worship. Not only had his natural sight been restored, but the eyes of his understanding had been opened. Christ had been revealed to his soul, and he received Him as the Sent of God.

A group of Pharisees had gathered near, and the sight of them brought to the mind of Jesus the contrast ever manifest in the effect of His words and works. He said, "For judgment I am come into this world, that they which see not might see; and that they which see might be made blind." Christ had come to open the blind eyes, to give light to them that sit in darkness. He had declared Himself to be the light of the world, and the miracle just performed was an attestation of His mission. The people who beheld the Saviour at His advent were favored with a fuller manifestation of the divine presence than the world had ever enjoyed before. The knowledge of God was revealed more perfectly. But in this very revelation, judgment was passing upon men. Their character was tested, their destiny determined.

The manifestation of divine power that had given to the blind man both natural and spiritual sight had left the Pharisees in yet deeper darkness. Some of His hearers, feeling that Christ's words applied to them, inquired, "Are we blind also?" Jesus answered, "If ye were blind, ye should have no sin." If God had made it impossible for you to see the truth, your ignorance would involve no guilt. "But now ye say, We see." You believe yourselves able to see, and reject the means through which alone you could receive sight. To all who realized their need, Christ came with infinite help. But the Pharisees would confess no need; they refused to come to Christ, and hence they were left in blindness,—a blindness for which they were themselves guilty. Jesus said, "Your sin remaineth."

13

The Divine Shepherd

This chapter is based on John 10:1-30.

I am the Good Shepherd: the good shepherd giveth his life for the sheep." "I am the Good Shepherd, and know My sheep, and am known of Mine. As the Father knoweth Me, even so know I the Father: and I lay down My life for the sheep."

Again Jesus found access to the minds of His hearers by the pathway of their familiar associations. He had likened the Spirit's influence to the cool, refreshing water. He had represented Himself as the light, the source of life and gladness to nature and to man. Now in a beautiful pastoral picture He represents His relation to those that believe on Him. No picture was more familiar to His hearers than this, and Christ's words linked it forever with Himself. Never could the disciples look on the shepherds tending their flocks without recalling the Saviour's lesson. They would see Christ in each faithful shepherd. They would see themselves in each helpless and dependent flock.

This figure the prophet Isaiah had applied to the Messiah's mission, in the comforting words, "O Zion, that bringest good tidings, get thee up into the high mountain; O Jerusalem, that bringest good tidings, lift up thy voice with strength; lift it up, be not afraid; say unto the cities of Judah, Behold your God! . . . He shall feed His flock like a shepherd: He shall gather the lambs with His arm, and carry them in His bosom." Isa. 40:9-11. David had sung, "The Lord is my shepherd; I shall not want." Ps. 23:1. And the Holy Spirit through Ezekiel had declared: "I will set up one Shepherd over them, and He shall feed them." "I will seek that which was lost, and bring again that which was driven away, and will bind up that which was broken, and will strengthen that which was sick." "And I will make with them a covenant of peace." "And they shall no more be a prey to the heathen; . . . but they shall dwell safely, and none shall make them afraid." Ezek. 34:23, 16, 25, 28.

Christ applied these prophecies to Himself, and He showed the contrast between His own character and that of the leaders in Israel. The Pharisees had just driven one from the fold, because he dared to bear witness to the power of Christ. They had cut off a soul whom the True Shepherd was drawing to Himself. In this they had shown themselves ignorant of the work committed to them, and unworthy of their trust as shepherds of the flock. Jesus now set before them the contrast between them and the Good Shepherd, and He pointed to Himself as the real keeper of the Lord's flock. Before doing this, however, He speaks of Himself under another figure.

He said, "He that entereth not by the door into the sheepfold, but climbeth up some other way, the same is a thief and a robber. But he that entereth in by the door is the shepherd of the sheep." The Pharisees did not discern that these words were spoken against them. When they reasoned in their hearts as to the meaning, Jesus told them plainly, "I am the door: by Me if any man enter in, he shall be saved, and shall go in and out, and find pasture. The thief cometh not, but for to steal, and to kill, and to destroy: I am come that they might have life, and that they might have it more abundantly."

Christ is the door to the fold of God. Through this door all His children, from the earliest times, have found entrance. In Jesus, as shown in types, as shadowed in symbols, as manifested in the revelation of the prophets, as unveiled in the lessons given to His disciples, and in the miracles wrought for the sons of men, they have beheld "the Lamb of God, which taketh away the sin of the world" (John 1:29), and through Him they are brought within the fold of His grace. Many have come presenting other objects for the faith of the world; ceremonies and systems have been devised by which men hope to receive justification and peace with God, and thus find entrance to His fold. But the only door is Christ, and all who have interposed something to take the place of Christ, all who have tried to enter the fold in some other way, are thieves and robbers.

The Pharisees had not entered by the door. They had climbed into the fold by another way than Christ, and they were not fulfilling the work of the true shepherd. The priests and rulers, the scribes and Pharisees, destroyed the living pastures, and defiled the wellsprings of the water of life. Faithfully do the words of inspiration describe those false shepherds: "The diseased have ye not strengthened, neither have ye healed that which was sick, neither have ye bound up that which was broken, neither have ye brought again that which was driven away; . . . but with force and with cruelty have ye ruled them." Ezek. 34:4.

In all ages, philosophers and teachers have been presenting to the world theories by which to satisfy the soul's need. Every heathen nation has had its great teachers and religious systems offering some other means of redemption than Christ, turning the eyes of men away from the Father's face, and filling their hearts with fear of Him who has given them only blessing. The trend of their work is to rob God of that which is His own, both by creation and by redemption. And these false teachers rob man as well. Millions of human beings are bound down under false religions, in the bondage of slavish fear, of stolid indifference, toiling like beasts of burden, bereft of hope or joy or aspiration here, and with only a dull fear of the hereafter. It is the gospel of the grace of God alone that can uplift the soul. The contemplation of the love of God manifested in His Son will stir the heart and arouse the powers of the soul as nothing else can. Christ came that He might re-create the image of God in man; and whoever turns men away from Christ is turning them away from the source of true development; he is defrauding them of the hope and purpose and glory of life. He is a thief and a robber.

"He that entereth in by the door is the shepherd of the sheep." Christ is both the door and the shepherd. He enters in by Himself. It is through His own sacrifice that He becomes the shepherd of the sheep. "To Him the porter openeth; and the sheep hear His voice: and He calleth His own sheep by name, and leadeth them out. And when He putteth forth His own sheep, He goeth before them, and the sheep follow Him: for they know His voice."

Of all creatures the sheep is one of the most timid and helpless, and in the East the shepherd's care for his flock is untiring and incessant. Anciently as now there was little security outside of the walled towns. Marauders from the roving border tribes, or beasts of prey from their hiding places in the rocks, lay in wait to plunder the flocks. The shepherd watched his charge, knowing that it was at the peril of his own life. Jacob, who kept the flocks of Laban in the pasture grounds of Haran, describing his own unwearied labor, said, "In the day the drought consumed me, and the frost by night; and my sleep departed from mine eyes." Gen. 31:40. And it was while guarding his father's sheep that the boy David, single-handed, encountered the lion and the bear, and rescued from their teeth the stolen lamb.

As the shepherd leads his flock over the rocky hills, through forest and wild ravines, to grassy nooks by the riverside; as he watches them on the mountains through the lonely night, shielding from robbers, caring tenderly for the sickly and feeble, his life comes to be one with theirs. A strong and tender attachment unites him to the objects of his care. However large the flock, the shepherd knows every sheep. Every one has its name, and responds to the name at the shepherd's call.

As an earthly shepherd knows his sheep, so does the divine Shepherd know His flock that are scattered throughout the world. "Ye My flock, the flock of My pasture, are men, and I am your God, saith the Lord God." Jesus says, "I have called thee by thy name; thou art Mine." "I have graven thee upon the palms of My hands." Ezek. 34:31; Isa. 43:1; 49:16.

Jesus knows us individually, and is touched with the feeling of our infirmities. He knows us all by name. He knows the very house in which we live, the name of each occupant. He has at times given directions to His servants to go to a certain street in a certain city, to such a house, to find one of His sheep.

Every soul is as fully known to Jesus as if he were the only one for whom the Saviour died. The distress of every one touches His heart. The cry for aid reaches His ear. He came to draw all men unto Himself. He bids them, "Follow Me," and His Spirit moves upon their hearts to draw them to come to Him. Many refuse to be drawn. Jesus knows who they are. He also knows who gladly hear His call, and are ready to come under His pastoral care. He says, "My sheep hear My voice, and I know them, and they follow Me." He cares for each one as if there were not another on the face of the earth.

"He calleth His own sheep by name, and leadeth them out. . . . And the sheep follow Him: for they know His voice." The Eastern shepherd does not drive his sheep. He depends not upon force or fear; but going before, he calls them. They know his voice, and obey the call. So does the Saviour-Shepherd with His sheep. The Scripture says, "Thou leddest Thy people like a flock by the hand of Moses and Aaron." Through the prophet, Jesus declares, "I have loved thee with an everlasting love: therefore with loving-kindness have I drawn thee." He compels none to follow Him. "I drew them," He says, "with cords of a man, with bands of love." Ps. 77:20; Jer. 31:3; Hosea 11:4.

It is not the fear of punishment, or the hope of everlasting reward, that leads the disciples of Christ to follow Him. They behold the Saviour's matchless love, revealed throughout His pilgrimage on earth, from the manger of Bethlehem to Calvary's cross, and the sight of Him attracts, it softens and subdues the soul. Love awakens in the heart of the beholders. They hear His voice, and they follow Him.

As the shepherd goes before his sheep, himself first encountering the perils of the way, so does Jesus with His people. "When He putteth forth His own sheep, He goeth before them." The way to heaven is consecrated by the Saviour's footprints. The path may be steep and rugged, but Jesus has traveled that way; His feet have pressed down the cruel thorns, to make the pathway easier for us. Every burden that we are called to bear He Himself has borne.

Though now He has ascended to the presence of God, and shares the throne of the universe, Jesus has lost none of His compassionate nature. Today the same tender, sympathizing heart is open to all the woes of humanity. Today the hand that was pierced is reached forth to bless more abundantly His people that are in the world. "And they shall never perish, neither shall any man pluck them out of My hand." The soul that has given himself to Christ is more precious in His sight than the whole world. The Saviour would have passed through the agony of Calvary that one might be saved in His kingdom. He will never abandon one for whom He has died. Unless His followers choose to leave Him, He will hold them fast.

Through all our trials we have a never-failing Helper. He does not leave us alone to struggle with temptation, to battle with evil, and be finally crushed with burdens and sorrow. Though now He is hidden from mortal sight, the ear of faith can hear His voice saying, Fear not; I am with you. "I am He that liveth, and was dead; and, behold, I am alive forevermore." Rev. 1:18. I have endured your sorrows, experienced your struggles, encountered your temptations. I know your tears; I also have wept. The griefs that lie too deep to be breathed into any human ear, I know. Think not that you are desolate and forsaken. Though your pain touch no responsive chord in any heart on earth, look unto Me, and live. "The mountains shall depart, and the hills be removed; but My kindness shall not depart from thee, neither shall the covenant of My peace be removed, saith the Lord that hath mercy on thee." Isa. 54:10.

However much a shepherd may love his sheep, he loves his sons and daughters more. Jesus is not only our shepherd; He is our "everlasting Father." And He says, "I know Mine own, and Mine own know Me, even as the Father knoweth Me, and I know the Father." John 10:14, 15, R. V. What a statement is this!—the only-begotten Son, He who is in the bosom of the Father, He whom God has declared to be "the Man that is My fellow" (Zech. 13:7),—the communion between Him and the eternal God is taken to represent the communion between Christ and His children on the earth!

Because we are the gift of His Father, and the reward of His work, Jesus loves us. He loves us as His children. Reader, He loves you. Heaven itself can bestow nothing greater, nothing better. Therefore trust.

Jesus thought upon the souls all over the earth who were misled by false shepherds. Those whom He longed to gather as the sheep of His pasture were scattered among wolves, and He said, "Other sheep I have, which are not of this fold: them also I must bring, and they shall hear My voice; and they shall become one flock, one shepherd." John 10:16, R. V.

"Therefore doth My Father love Me, because I lay down My life, that I might take it again." That is, My Father has so loved you, that He even loves Me more for giving My life to redeem you. In becoming your substitute and surety, by surrendering My life, by taking your liabilities, your transgressions, I am endeared to My Father.

"I lay down My life, that I might take it again. No man taketh it from Me, but I lay it down of Myself. I have power to lay it down, and I have power to take it again." While as a member of the human family He was mortal, as God He was the fountain of life for the world. He could have withstood the advances of death, and refused to come under its dominion; but voluntarily He laid down His life, that He might bring life and immortality to light. He bore the sin of the world, endured its curse, yielded up His life as a sacrifice, that men might not eternally die. "Surely He hath borne our griefs, and carried our sorrows. . . . He was wounded for our transgressions, He was bruised for our iniquities: the chastisement of our peace was upon Him; and with His stripes we are healed. All we like sheep have gone astray; we have turned every one to his own way; and the Lord hath laid on Him the iniquity of us all." Isa. 53:4-6.

14

The Last Journey From Galilee

This chapter is based on Luke 9:51-56; 10:1-24.

As the close of His ministry drew near, there was a change in Christ's manner of labor. Heretofore He had sought to shun excitement and publicity. He had refused the homage of the people, and had passed quickly from place to place when the popular enthusiasm in His favor seemed kindling beyond control. Again and again He had commanded that none should declare Him to be the Christ.

At the time of the Feast of Tabernacles His journey to Jerusalem was made swiftly and secretly. When urged by His brothers to present Himself publicly as the Messiah, His answer was, "My time is not yet come." John 7:6. He made His way to Jerusalem unobserved, and entered the city unannounced, and unhonored by the multitude. But not so with His last journey. He had left Jerusalem for a season because of the malice of the priests and rabbis. But He now set out to return, traveling in the most public manner, by a circuitous route, and preceded by such an announcement of His coming as He had never made before. He was going forward to the scene of His great sacrifice, and to this the attention of the people must be directed.

"As Moses lifted up the serpent in the wilderness, even so must the Son of man be lifted up." John 3:14. As the eyes of all Israel had been directed to the uplifted serpent, the symbol appointed for their healing, so all eyes must be drawn to Christ, the sacrifice that brought salvation to the lost world.

It was a false conception of the Messiah's work, and a lack of faith in the divine character of Jesus, that had led His brothers to urge Him to present Himself publicly to the people at the Feast of Tabernacles. Now, in a spirit akin to this, the disciples would have prevented Him from making the journey to Jerusalem. They remembered His words concerning what was to befall Him there, they knew the deadly hostility of the religious leaders, and they would fain have dissuaded their Master from going thither.

To the heart of Christ it was a bitter task to press His way against the fears, disappointment, and unbelief of His beloved disciples. It was hard to lead them forward to the anguish and despair that awaited them at Jerusalem. And Satan was at hand to press his temptations upon the Son of man. Why should He now go to Jerusalem, to certain death? All around Him were souls hungering for the bread of life. On every hand were suffering ones waiting for His word of healing. The work to be wrought by the gospel of His grace was but just begun. And He was full of the vigor of manhood's prime. Why not go forward to the vast fields of the world with the words of His grace, the touch of His healing power? Why not take to Himself the joy of giving light and gladness to those darkened and sorrowing millions? Why leave the harvest gathering to His disciples, so weak in faith, so dull of understanding, so slow to act? Why face death now, and leave the work in its infancy? The foe who in the wilderness had confronted Christ assailed Him now with fierce and subtle temptations. Had Jesus yielded for a moment, had He changed His course in the least particular to save Himself, Satan's agencies would have triumphed, and the world would have been lost.

But Jesus had "steadfastly set His face to go to Jerusalem." The one law of His life was the Father's will. In the visit to the temple in His boyhood, He had said to Mary, "Wist ye not that I must be about My Father's business?" Luke 2:49. At Cana, when Mary desired Him to reveal His miraculous power, His answer was, "Mine hour is not yet come." John 2:4. With the same words He replied to His brothers when they urged Him to go to the feast. But in God's great plan the hour had been appointed for the offering of Himself for the sins of men, and that hour was soon to strike. He would not fail nor falter. His steps are turned toward Jerusalem, where His foes have long plotted to take His life; now He will lay it down. He set His face steadfastly to go to persecution, denial, rejection, condemnation, and death.

And He "sent messengers before His face: and they went, and entered into a village of the Samaritans, to make ready for Him." But the people refused to receive Him, because He was on His way to Jerusalem. This they interpreted as meaning that Christ showed a preference for the Jews, whom they hated with intense bitterness. Had He come to restore the temple and worship upon Mount Gerizim, they would gladly have received Him; but He was going to Jerusalem, and they would show Him no hospitality. Little did they realize that they were turning from their doors the best gift of heaven. Jesus invited men to receive Him, He asked favors at their hands, that He might come near to them, to bestow the richest blessings. For every favor manifested toward Him, He requited a more precious grace. But all was lost to the Samaritans because of their prejudice and bigotry.

James and John, Christ's messengers, were greatly annoyed at the insult shown to their Lord. They were filled with indignation because He had been so rudely treated by the Samaritans whom He was honoring by His presence. They had recently been with Him on the mount of transfiguration, and had seen Him glorified by God, and honored by Moses and Elijah. This manifest dishonor on the part of the Samaritans, should not, they thought, be passed over without marked punishment.

Coming to Christ, they reported to Him the words of the people, telling Him that they had even refused to give Him a night's lodging. They thought that a grievous wrong had been done Him, and seeing Mount Carmel in the distance, where Elijah had slain the false prophets, they said, "Wilt Thou that we command fire to come down from heaven, and consume them, even as Elias did?" They were surprised to see that Jesus was pained by their words, and still more surprised as His rebuke fell upon their ears, "Ye know not what manner of spirit ye are of. For the Son of man is not come to destroy men's lives, but to save them." And He went to another village.

It is no part of Christ's mission to compel men to receive Him.

It is Satan, and men actuated by his spirit, that seek to compel the conscience. Under a pretense of zeal for righteousness, men who are confederate with evil angels bring suffering upon their fellow men, in order to convert them to their ideas of religion; but Christ is ever showing mercy, ever seeking to win by the revealing of His love. He can admit no rival in the soul, nor accept of partial service; but He desires only voluntary service, the willing surrender of the heart under the constraint of love. There can be no more conclusive evidence that we possess the spirit of Satan than the disposition to hurt and destroy those who do not appreciate our work, or who act contrary to our ideas.

Every human being, in body, soul, and spirit, is the property of God. Christ died to redeem all. Nothing can be more offensive to God than for men, through religious bigotry, to bring suffering upon those who are the purchase of the Saviour's blood.

"And He arose from thence, and cometh into the coasts of Judea by the farther side of Jordan: and the people resort unto Him again; and, as He was wont, He taught them again." Mark 10:1.

A considerable part of the closing months of Christ's ministry was spent in Perea, the province on "the farther side of Jordan" from Judea. Here the multitude thronged His steps, as in His early ministry in Galilee, and much of His former teaching was repeated.

As He had sent out the twelve, so He "appointed seventy others, and sent them two and two before His face into every city and place, whither He Himself was about to come." Luke 10:1, R. V. These disciples had been for some time with Him, in training for their work. When the twelve were sent out on their first separate mission, other disciples accompanied Jesus in His journey through Galilee. Thus they had the privilege of intimate association with Him, and direct personal instruction. Now this larger number also were to go forth on a separate mission.

The directions to the seventy were similar to those that had been given to the twelve; but the command to the twelve, not to enter into any city of the Gentiles or of the Samaritans, was not given to the seventy. Though Christ had just been repulsed by the Samaritans, His love toward them was unchanged. When the seventy went forth in His name, they visited, first of all, the cities of Samaria.

The Saviour's own visit to Samaria, and later, the commendation of the good Samaritan, and the grateful joy of that leper, a Samaritan, who alone of the ten returned to give thanks to Christ, were full of significance to the disciples. The lesson sank deep into their hearts. In His commission to them, just before His ascension, Jesus mentioned Samaria with Jerusalem and Judea as the places where they were first to preach the gospel. This commission His teaching had prepared them to fulfill. When in their Master's name they went to Samaria, they found the people ready to receive them. The Samaritans had heard of Christ's words of commendation and His works of mercy for men of their nation. They saw that, notwithstanding their rude treatment of Him, He had only thoughts of love toward them, and their hearts were won. After His ascension they welcomed the Saviour's messengers, and the disciples gathered a precious harvest from among those who had once been their bitterest enemies. "A bruised reed shall He not break, and the dimly burning flax shall He not quench: He shall bring forth judgment unto truth." "And in His name shall the Gentiles trust." Isa. 42:3, margin; Matt. 12:21.

In sending out the seventy, Jesus bade them, as He had bidden the twelve, not to urge their presence where they were unwelcome. "Into whatsoever city ye enter, and they receive you not," He said, "go your ways out into the streets of the same, and say, Even the very dust of your city, which cleaveth on us, we do wipe off against you: notwithstanding be ye sure of this, that the kingdom of God is come nigh unto you." They were not to do this from motives of resentment or through wounded dignity, but to show how grievous a thing it is to refuse the Lord's message or His messengers. To reject the Lord's servants is to reject Christ Himself.

"I say unto you," Jesus added, "that it shall be more tolerable in that day for Sodom, than for that city." Then His mind reverted to the Galilean towns where so much of His ministry had been spent. In deeply sorrowful accents He exclaimed, "Woe unto thee, Chorazin! woe unto thee, Bethsaida! for if the mighty works had been done in Tyre and Sidon, which have been done in you, they had a great while ago repented, sitting in sackcloth and ashes. But it shall be more tolerable for Tyre and Sidon at the judgment, than for you. And thou, Capernaum, which art exalted to heaven, shalt be thrust down to hell."

To those busy towns about the Sea of Galilee, heaven's richest blessings had been freely offered. Day after day the Prince of life had gone in and out among them. The glory of God, which prophets and kings had longed to see, had shone upon the multitudes that thronged the Saviour's steps. Yet they had refused the heavenly Gift.

With a great show of prudence the rabbis had warned the people against receiving the new doctrines taught by this new teacher; for His theories and practices were contrary to the teachings of the fathers. The people gave credence to what the priests and Pharisees taught, in place of seeking to understand the word of God for themselves. They honored the priests and rulers instead of honoring God, and rejected the truth that they might keep their own traditions. Many had been impressed and almost persuaded; but they did not act upon their convictions, and were not reckoned on the side of Christ. Satan presented his temptations, until the light appeared as darkness. Thus many rejected the truth that would have proved the saving of the soul.

The True Witness says, "Behold, I stand at the door, and knock." Rev. 3:20. Every warning, reproof, and entreaty in the word of God or through His messengers is a knock at the door of the heart. It is the voice of Jesus asking for entrance. With every knock unheeded, the disposition to open becomes weaker. The impressions of the Holy Spirit if disregarded today, will not be as strong tomorrow. The heart becomes less impressible, and lapses into a perilous unconsciousness of the shortness of life, and of the great eternity beyond. Our condemnation in the judgment will not result from the fact that we have been in error, but from the fact that we have neglected heaven-sent opportunities for learning what is truth.

Like the apostles, the seventy had received supernatural endowments as a seal of their mission. When their work was completed, they returned with joy, saying, "Lord, even the devils are subject unto us through Thy name." Jesus answered, "I beheld Satan as lightning fall from heaven."

The scenes of the past and the future were presented to the mind of Jesus. He beheld Lucifer as he was first cast out from the heavenly places. He looked forward to the scenes of His own agony, when before all the worlds the character of the deceiver should be unveiled. He heard the cry, "It is finished" (John 19:30), announcing that the redemption of the lost race was forever made certain, that heaven was made eternally secure against the accusations, the deceptions, the pretensions, that Satan would instigate.

Beyond the cross of Calvary, with its agony and shame, Jesus looked forward to the great final day, when the prince of the power of the air will meet his destruction in the earth so long marred by his rebellion. Jesus beheld the work of evil forever ended, and the peace of God filling heaven and earth.

Henceforward Christ's followers were to look upon Satan as a conquered foe. Upon the cross, Jesus was to gain the victory for them; that victory He desired them to accept as their own. "Behold," He said, "I give unto you power to tread on serpents and scorpions, and over all the power of the enemy: and nothing shall by any means hurt you."

The omnipotent power of the Holy Spirit is the defense of every contrite soul. Not one that in penitence and faith has claimed His protection will Christ permit to pass under the enemy's power. The Saviour is by the side of His tempted and tried ones. With Him there can be no such thing as failure, loss, impossibility, or defeat; we can do all things through Him who strengthens us. When temptations and trials come, do not wait to adjust all the difficulties, but look to Jesus, your helper.

There are Christians who think and speak altogether too much about the power of Satan. They think of their adversary, they pray about him, they talk about him, and he looms up greater and greater in their imagination. It is true that Satan is a powerful being; but, thank God, we have a mighty Saviour, who cast out the evil one from heaven. Satan is pleased when we magnify his power. Why not talk of Jesus? Why not magnify His power and His love?

The rainbow of promise encircling the throne on high is an everlasting testimony that "God so loved the world, that He gave His only-begotten Son, that whosoever believeth in Him should not perish, but have everlasting life." John 3:16. It testifies to the universe that God will never forsake His people in their struggle with evil. It is an assurance to us of strength and protection as long as the throne itself shall endure.

Jesus added, "Notwithstanding in this rejoice not, that the spirits are subject unto you; but rather rejoice, because your names are written in heaven." Rejoice not in the possession of power, lest you lose sight of your dependence upon God. Be careful lest self-sufficiency come in, and you work in your own strength, rather than in the spirit and strength of your Master. Self is ever ready to take the credit if any measure of success attends the work. Self is flattered and exalted, and the impression is not made upon other minds that God is all and in all. The apostle Paul says, "When I am weak, then am I strong." 2 Cor. 12:10. When we have a realization of our weakness, we learn to depend upon a power not inherent. Nothing can take so strong a hold on the heart as the abiding sense of our responsibility to God. Nothing reaches so fully down to the deepest motives of conduct as a sense of the pardoning love of Christ. We are to come in touch with God, then we shall be imbued with His Holy Spirit, that enables us to come in touch with our fellow men. Then rejoice that through Christ you have become connected with God, members of the heavenly family. While you look higher than yourself, you will have a continual sense of the weakness of humanity. The less you cherish self, the more distinct and full will be your comprehension of the excellence of your Saviour. The more closely you connect yourself with the source of light and power, the greater light will be shed upon you, and the greater power will be yours to work for God. Rejoice that you are one with God, one with Christ, and with the whole family of heaven.

As the seventy listened to the words of Christ, the Holy Spirit was impressing their minds with living realities, and writing truth upon the tablets of the soul. Though multitudes surrounded them, they were as though shut in with God.

Knowing that they had caught the inspiration of the hour, Jesus "rejoiced in spirit, and said, I thank Thee, O Father, Lord of heaven and earth, that Thou hast hid these things from the wise and prudent, and hast revealed them unto babes: even so, Father; for so it seemed good in Thy sight. All things are delivered to Me of My Father: and no man knoweth who the Son is, but the Father, and who the Father is, but the Son, and he to whom the Son will reveal Him."

The honored men of the world, the so-called great and wise men, with all their boasted wisdom, could not comprehend the character of Christ. They judged Him from outward appearance, from the humiliation that came upon Him as a human being. But to fishermen and publicans it had been given to see the Invisible. Even the disciples failed of understanding all that Jesus desired to reveal to them; but from time to time, as they surrendered themselves to the Holy Spirit's power, their minds were illuminated. They realized that the mighty God, clad in the garb of humanity, was among them. Jesus rejoiced that though this knowledge was not possessed by the wise and prudent, it had been revealed to these humble men. Often as He had presented the Old Testament Scriptures, and showed their application to Himself and His work of atonement, they had been awakened by His Spirit, and lifted into a heavenly atmosphere. Of the spiritual truths spoken by the prophets they had a clearer understanding than had the original writers themselves. Hereafter they would read the Old Testament Scriptures, not as the doctrines of the scribes and Pharisees, not as the utterances of wise men who were dead, but as a new revelation from God. They beheld Him "whom the world cannot receive, because it seeth Him not, neither knoweth Him: but ye know Him; for He dwelleth with you, and shall be in you." John 14:17.

The only way in which we can gain a more perfect apprehension of truth is by keeping the heart tender and subdued by the Spirit of Christ. The soul must be cleansed from vanity and pride, and vacated of all that has held it in possession, and Christ must be enthroned within. Human science is too limited to comprehend the atonement. The plan of redemption is so far-reaching that philosophy cannot explain it. It will ever remain a mystery that the most profound reasoning cannot fathom. The science of salvation cannot be explained; but it can be known by experience. Only he who sees his own sinfulness can discern the preciousness of the Saviour.

Full of instruction were the lessons which Christ taught as He slowly made His way from Galilee toward Jerusalem. Eagerly the people listened to His words. In Perea as in Galilee the people were less under the control of Jewish bigotry than in Judea, and His teaching found a response in their hearts.

During these last months of His ministry, many of Christ's parables were spoken. The priests and rabbis pursued Him with ever-increasing bitterness, and His warnings to them He veiled in symbols. They could not mistake His meaning, yet they could find in His words nothing on which to ground an accusation against Him. In the parable of the Pharisee and the publican, the self-sufficient prayer, "God, I thank Thee that I am not as the rest of men," stood out in sharp contrast to the penitent's plea, "Be merciful to me the sinner." Luke 18:11, 13, R. V., margin. Thus Christ rebuked the hypocrisy of the Jews. And under the figures of the barren fig tree and the great supper He foretold the doom about to fall upon the impenitent nation. Those who had scornfully rejected the invitation to the gospel feast heard His warning words: "I say unto you, That none of those men which were bidden shall taste of My supper." Luke 14:24.

Very precious was the instruction given to the disciples. The parable of the importunate widow and the friend asking for bread at midnight gave new force to His words, "Ask, and it shall be given you; seek, and ye shall find; knock, and it shall be opened unto you." Luke 11:9. And often their wavering faith was strengthened by the memory that Christ had said, "Shall not God do justice for His elect, which cry to Him day and night, and He is long-suffering over them? I say unto you, that He will do them justice speedily." Luke 18:7, 8, R. V., margin.

The beautiful parable of the lost sheep Christ repeated. And He carried its lesson still farther, as He told of the lost piece of silver and the prodigal son. The force of these lessons the disciples could not then fully appreciate; but after the outpouring of the Holy Spirit, as they saw the ingathering of the Gentiles and the envious anger of the Jews, they better understood the lesson of the prodigal son, and could enter into the joy of Christ's words, "It was meet that we should make merry, and be glad;" "for this my son was dead, and is alive again; he was lost, and is found." Luke 15:32, 24. And as they went out in their Master's name, facing reproach and poverty and persecution, they often strengthened their hearts by repeating His injunction, spoken on this last journey, "Fear not, little flock; for it is your Father's good pleasure to give you the kingdom. Sell that ye have, and give alms; provide yourselves bags which wax not old, a treasure in the heavens that faileth not, where no thief approacheth, neither moth corrupteth. For where your treasure is, there will your heart be also." Luke 12:32-34.

Scriptural Index